TERRORISM, HUMAN RIGHTS, AND THE CASE FOR WORLD GOVERNMENT

TERRORISM, HUMAN RIGHTS, AND THE CASE FOR WORLD GOVERNMENT

Louis P. Pojman

ROWMAN & LITTLEFIELD PUBLISHERS, INC.
Lanham • Boulder • New York • Toronto • Oxford

ROWMAN & LITTLEFIELD PUBLISHERS, INC.

Published in the United States of America
by Rowman & Littlefield Publishers, Inc.
A wholly owned subsidary of The Rowman & Littlefield Publishing Group, Inc.
4501 Forbes Boulevard, Suite 200, Lanham, Maryland 20706
www.rowmanlittlefield.com

PO Box 317
Oxford
OX2 9RU, UK

British Library Cataloguing in Publication Information Available

Library of Congress Cataloging-in-Publication Data

Pojman, Louis P.
  Terrorism, human rights, and the case for world government / Louis P. Pojman.
      p. cm.
  Includes bibliographical references.
  ISBN-13: 978-0-7425-5160-2 (cloth : alk. paper)
  ISBN-10: 0-7425-5160-1 (cloth : alk. paper)
  1. International organization. 2. Terrorism—Prevention. 3. Human rights. I. Title.
  JZ1318.P63 2006
  341.2'1—dc22   2006004559

♾™ The paper used in this publication meets the minimum requirements of
American National Standard for Information Sciences—Permanence of Paper
for Printed Library Materials, ANSI/NISO Z39.48-1992.

Dedicated to the memory of Louis Paul Pojman, and to all those who will continue to use the power of ideas and morally directed action to bring mutual understanding, peace, and justice to our world.

Contents

Preface

Ideas of economic and political philosophers both when they are
right and when they are wrong are more powerful than is commonly
understood. Indeed, the world is ruled by little else. Madmen in authority, who hear voices in the air, are distilling their frenzy from
some academic scribbler of a few years back. . . . Sooner or later it is
ideas, not vested interests, which are dangerous for good or evil.[1]

—John Maynard Keynes

M Y THESIS IS THAT BOTH GLOBALISM with all its accompanying promises and problems plus cogent moral arguments for cosmopolitanism are moving us toward the need for greater international cooperation, based on enforceable international law. I argue that the best way
to realize these globalist and moral goals is through the establishment of
a world government. I develop this thesis within a Hobbesian framework, which views the multitude of nations as existing in a state of
global anarchy.

As this preface is being written there is violent expression of a conflict
of ideas and their relationship to each other in the area of human rights
as they relate to freedom of expression and open discussion versus perceived disrespect for the values and beliefs of another cultural and religious group.[2] Western values reflect the legacy of Socrates and are com-
fortable with difference and inconclusiveness as ways of approaching

deepened understanding; deviations from those values are eventually corrected over time. Exaggerated, purist versions of beliefs, whether Muslim or from another religion or value system, do not allow for such open expression and dialogue. The need to reassert the use of the power of ideas for good has never been greater.

The first chapter describes the effect of the growing menace of non-state terrorism on people everywhere. I distinguish *Old-Style* from *New-Style* terrorism. *Old-Style* terrorists, such as the Jewish zealots of the first century C.E., the Jewish Stern Gang, the PLO, and the Baader-Meinhof Gang have generally confined themselves to specific targets and avoided harming "innocent people." *New-Style* terrorists raise the level of violence and reject the distinction between combatants and civilians. The hallmark of *New-Style* terrorism is the suicide bomber, epitomized in the attacks on the World Trade Center and the London Underground, willing to kill both him- or herself and others in order to spread death and chaos, and typically considering him- or herself an altruist rather than a fanatic. I conclude by suggesting ways of combating terrorism.

Chapter 2 examines the virtues and vices of nationalism, comparing the results with the promises and problems of cosmopolitanism and concluding that something like soft nationalism, where states enjoy limited but not total sovereignty, is compatible with a form of democratic cosmopolitanism or limited world government. First I show how various aspects of globalism are bringing humanity closer together and then bolster the globalist tendencies toward a centralized managerial institution with two moral arguments that justify a preference for institutionalized cosmopolitanism over nationalism. I outline my theory of *soft nationalism* and show that it is compatible with a republican form of world government. Finally, I defend my theory against several objections, including those of Kant, Rawls, and Gregory Kaftka.

In chapter 3, I describe how universal human rights were formulated in The Declaration approved by the United Nations in 1946 under the leadership of Eleanor Roosevelt and argue that human rights are ultimately grounded in universal duties. I show that while duties have a wider scope than rights and are able to ground them, the reverse is not true and develop an overall justification of human rights, one holding that they are correlative to moral duties. After meeting objections against the universal rights/duties thesis I conclude that universal human rights will be the glue that holds humanity together, protecting people from oppression and enabling them to live worthwhile lives.

A brief discussion of cosmopolitanism closes this work. I outline some possible routes to the actualization of world government, and close on a hopeful note.

I will undoubtedly miss thanking some who gave generously of their time to read and critique the several versions of this work, and can only trust they will understand. Robert Audi, Sterling Harwood, Jonathan Harrison, Tziporah Kasachkoff, Steven Kersner, Jim Landesman, Jim Janes, Ruth Pojman, Martin Schonfeld, and Walter P. Sinnott-Armstrong made suggestions on improving earlier drafts of this work. Eve DeVaro was the initial acquisitions editor; Ross Miller succeeded her and continued to be supportive as the book went on to production. Emily Ross, editorial assistant; Karen Ackermann, associate production editor; and Meghann French, copy editor, all ensured that the manuscript and supporting materials were properly prepared. I would also like to thank William Cornwell, Mary Gilbertson, Hugh LaFollette, Morton Winston, and Joseph Runzo. Deep appreciation is expressed to each one. In addition, thanks is due to participants in the faculty seminars of the Department of English and Philosophy at the U.S. Military Academy at West Point, New York; in the International Kant Conference held in November 2004 at Allameh Tabatabaii University in Tehran, Iran; and to graduate students and Fellows at Clare Hall, Cambridge University, U.K., 2004–2005.

Earlier versions of the ideas presented in this work appeared in the following publications: *Terrorism and International Justice*, Jim Sterba, ed. (Oxford University Press, 2003), used here with permission; *Justice, an Anthology*, Louis P. Pojman, ed., "Foundations of Philosophy Series," (Pearson/Prentice-Hall, 2006); and the *Croatian Journal of Philosophy* 4, no. 10 (2004).

Louis Pojman learned that this work was accepted for publication about three weeks before he died, on October 15, 2005. This preface, written posthumously by Trudy, his wife of forty-three years, is based in part on an abstract he wrote. Louis told me and our children, Ruth Freedom and Paul Theodore, that he considered this book and the vision it holds out for a better future the most important thing he had written. Philosophy is an exciting subject that holds ideas as a high value. We,

Louis Pojman's wife and children, hope that you the reader will be inspired to discuss his ideas and do your part to ensure that the most dangerous, powerful ideas are good ones that will contribute to furthering global peace and justice.

Louis P. Pojman and Gertrude "Trudy" Pojman
February 10, 2006

Notes

1. John Maynard Keynes (1883–1946), British economist. *The General Theory of Employment, Interest and Money*, chapter 24 (1936).

2. This reference is to the current violence and debate over publication of cartoons of the Prophet Muhammad in the Danish newspaper *Jyllands-Posten* in October 2005.

1

The Moral Response to Terrorism and the Cosmopolitan Imperative[1]

And when the sacred months are passed, kill those who join other gods with God wherever ye shall find them; and seize them, and lay wait for them with every kind of ambush. . . . Strive against [jihad] the infidels [*kafir*] and the hypocrites! Be harsh with them. Their ultimate destiny is hell.

—Qur'an 9:3

IN THIS CHAPTER I WILL FIRST DISCUSS the attacks of September 11, 2001, in light of international terrorism, distinguish old-style from new-style terrorism, and then discuss short-term and long-term moral responses to it, defending a cosmopolitan perspective.

Introduction: The Day of Ignominy

On September 11, 2001, the worst terrorist attack on civilians in the history of the United States occurred. Four planes, hijacked by Arab Muslim terrorists, became massive, murderous missiles in their hands. Two of them crashed into New York City's World Trade Center, another crashed into the Pentagon in Washington, D.C., and a fourth, perhaps headed for the Capitol building, crashed into a Pennsylvania field. More than three thousand unsuspecting, innocent people were killed, as were the nineteen terrorists. The horrendous kamikaze attacks destroyed a symbol of global capitalism and dented the military headquarters of the most powerful military force on Earth. This diabolical carousel of contempt and contumely was not an attack just on the United States but on the West, and on the liberal culture and values it embodies. These lethal suicidal missiles created a gaping hole in a seemingly impregnable wall of civilization, disabusing us of our illusions of invulnerability. We now glimpse through the "hole of hell" the menacing brutal barbarism on the other side of the wall. The attack, with its attending "hole in the wall," seemed aimed ultimately at *her* august torch. Thus a new era in human history was inaugurated, one that portends a new dimension of evil and a different type of war. The history of the United States and the entire world will henceforth be divided into Before 9/11 and After 9/11.

Since that ominous day in 2001, several other terrorist bombings have occurred. On October 12, 2002, 202 people were killed in a hotel bombing in Bali, Indonesia. In November 2003, terrorists detonated bombs outside the British consulate in Istanbul, Turkey, killing 23 and wounding many others. In March 2004, terrorists detonated ten bombs on trains in Madrid, Spain, killing 191 people. In the latest incidents, on July 7, 2005, four young British Muslim suicide bombers detonated three bombs on the London Underground and one on a bus, killing some 50 people and wounding 700.

Iraqi insurgents detonate bombs in Baghdad and the Sunni triangle almost daily, killing or maiming thousands of innocent Iraqis, including pensioners, women, and children. For example, on July 13, 2005, a suicide bomber drove his bomb-laden truck into a crowd of children who were receiving candy from a soldier. Twenty-five people were killed, mostly children. In the past two years more Iraqis have been killed by terrorist attacks than by American and British forces. Contractors, nongovernmental organization (NGO) workers, diplomats, and journalists have been beheaded, usually by terrorist groups linked to al Qaeda. A report issued in Iraq on July 19, 2005, stated that twenty-five thousand civilians had been killed in the previous two years: 37 percent by US and UK forces; 46 percent by Iraqi criminals and insurgents (terrorists).

Let us provisionally define *terrorism* broadly as "using violence against innocents for political or military purposes." As such, terrorism is not new, of course. In the 1980s, 5,431 international terrorist incidents occurred in which 4,684 people died; in the 1990s, 3,824 incidents occurred, with 2,468 deaths. From 1970 to 1995, 64,319 terrorist incidents were recorded, half of them attributed to religious extremists.[2] If one includes state-sponsored terrorism, the twentieth century will be hard to equal in terms of terrorist atrocities. It is estimated that governments worldwide killed 169 million of their own people between 1900 and 1987. Joseph Stalin, the all-time megamurderer, accounts for about 43 million deaths; Mao Tse-tung, 38 million; and Adolf Hitler, 21 million.[3]

Many nations and groups have practiced terrorism in the past fifty years. The United States has supported and trained terrorist groups such as the contras in Nicaragua and the mujahideen in Afghanistan. The African National Congress, led by Nelson Mandela, used terrorist tactics to force the government of white South Africa to end apartheid. Northern Ireland and England have had to endure the terrorist threats of the Irish Republican Army (IRA) for decades, and Israel has had to live with suicide bombings for years. Indeed, Israel, though the target of some of the worst terrorist attacks in history, shares the responsibility for the onset of modern terror. Seeking to drive the British from Palestine, the Zionist militant groups Irgun (also known as Etzel) and the Stern Gang were early perpetrators of terrorist violence in the Middle East. On July 22, 1946, the Polish Jew Menachem Begin, later to become prime minister of Israel, led a group of Etzel saboteurs into the kitchen of the King David Hotel in Jerusalem, which served as the headquarters of British governmental offices. They deposited milk cans packed with gelignite in the hotel's lower floor, set the fuses, and fled. When the explosion occurred twenty-five minutes later, 91 people—British, Arab, and Jewish—were killed and 45 injured. On April 9, 1948, the Stern Gang invaded and captured the Arab village of Deir Yassim, killing more than 230 Arab men, women, and children, mutilating their bodies.[4] Israel, it might be argued, was itself founded on terror and continues to vie with the Palestinians for that dishonorable label. Yet instead of calling Israel a terrorist state, the United States funds it to the tune of more than $3 billion per year.

But no group has relied on terrorist actions more than those connected with the Palestinian movement in Israel, such as the Popular Front for the Liberation of Palestine (PFLP) and the Palestine Liberation Organization (PLO), who have used terrorist tactics in a number of airline hijackings (especially between 1968 and 1972), the murder of eleven Israeli Olympic athletes in September 1972 by the group Black September, and the spate of suicide bombings against civilians since 1996. One of the worst incidents was the suicide bombing at a March 2002 Passover Seder in Tel Aviv that killed twenty-six Israelis and wounded a hundred more. Thanks to ample media coverage, these tactics have gotten the attention of the world and brought significant benefits to the Palestinian cause, including the United Nations' (UN) decision to grant observer status to the PLO in 1974 and later recognition of the right of Palestinians to a state, as well as a Nobel Peace Prize for Yasser Arafat in 1994. Arafat has received invitations to speak at the best universities in the West, including Oxford and Harvard, and an honorary doctorate from Maastricht University in 1999. The European Economic Community endorsed Palestinian statehood in 1980, and even US president George W. Bush has called for a Palestinian state. The Palestinians may deserve a state, but other people who may also merit self-determination, such as Turkish Kurds and Chinese Uighurs, have not galvanized world attention in the way the Palestinians have. George Habash and other terrorist leaders have frankly admitted that they owe their attention-getting success to terrorism. Terrorism pays. As Habash has noted, "When we hijack a plane it has more effect than if we killed a hundred Israelis in battle."[5] The PLO's chief observer at the UN noted that "[t]he first several hijackings [accomplished more for the Palestinian cause] than twenty years of pleading at the United Nations."[6]

There is a long history of terrorism in the Middle East that the Palestinians terrorists may simply be continuing. Let us begin by defining the term.

Definition of Terrorism

Terrorism is a type of political violence that intentionally targets civilians (noncombatants) in a ruthlessly destructive, often unpredictable manner. Terrorism hardly constitutes mindless violence. Instead, it reflects a detailed strategy that uses horrific violence to make people feel weak and vulnerable, often disproportionately to either the terrorist act or to the terrorists' long-term power. This undermining fear is then utilized to promote concrete political objectives. While some of these objectives may be morally commendable, their moral quality tends to be annulled by the murderous means employed, so that terrorism must be discouraged by civilized governments. Essentially, terrorism employs *horrific violence against unsuspecting civilians, as well as combatants, in order to inspire fear and create panic, which in turn will advance the terrorists' political or religious agenda.* Although this definition can be qualified and refined, it will serve my purposes in this chapter.

Hama Rules: The Background Metaphor for the Terrorism of September 11

In his book *From Beirut to Jerusalem*, Thomas Friedman describes atrocities that took place in Hama, Syria, in early February of 1982. After an assassination attempt on Syrian president Hafez Assad was traced to the Muslim Brotherhood, a group of Sunni Muslim militants in the town of Hama, Assad's forces, led by his brother Rifaat, launched an attack on the Brotherhood in Hama. A fierce civil war broke out between the Muslim guerillas and the Syrian military. Prisoners were tortured and buildings, even mosques, were destroyed. After a few weeks much of Hama was in rubble. Assad brought in bulldozers to flatten rubble. Between seven and thirty-eight thousand people were killed. "Normally, a politician would play down such a ghastly incident and dismiss the high casualty numbers as the enemy's propaganda, but Assad's forces claimed them as a badge of honor."

Friedman argues that the incident illustrates the rules of Arab warfare, "Hama Rules," which come straight out of a Hobbesian state of nature, where life is "solitary, poor, nasty, brutish, and short." Destroy or be destroyed! Warring tribes confront each other with no impartial arbiter to enforce mutually agreed-upon rules, so the only relevant concern is survival, which entails that the enemy must be destroyed by whatever means necessary. Friedman describes the Middle Eastern states as brutal autocracies where leaders (despots) like Assad and former Iraqi president Saddam Hussein survived by oppressive tactics, including framing their enemies, and torturing and executing political rivals. "Restraint and magnanimity are luxuries of the self-confident, and the rulers of these countries are anything but secure on their thrones," writes Friedman.[7]

Friedman illustrates his theory with a Bedouin legend about an old man and his turkey. One day an elderly Bedouin discovered that by eating turkey he could restore his virility. He bought a small turkey and kept it around his tent, feeding it so that it would provide a source of renewed strength. One day the turkey was stolen. So the Bedouin called his sons together and said, "Boys, my turkey has been stolen. We are in danger now." His sons laughed, replying, "Father, it's no big deal. What do you need a turkey for?" "Never mind," the father replied. "We must get the turkey back." But his sons didn't take this seriously and soon forgot about the turkey. A few weeks later the Bedouin's sons came to him and said, "Father, our camel has been stolen. What should we do?" "Find my turkey," the Bedouin replied. A few weeks later the sons came to him again, saying that the old man's horse had been stolen. "Find my turkey," he responded. Finally, a few weeks after that, someone raped his daughter. The Bedouin gazed at his sons and said, "It's all because of the turkey. When they saw that they could take away my turkey, we lost everything."[8]

To let your enemy take an inch is to give him a mile; it is to lose your wealth, your status, your reputation, your integrity. In such a state the rule is not "an eye for an eye, a tooth for a tooth, a life for life," but "a life for an eye, two for a tooth, and the lives of your entire tribe for the life of my turkey." Friedman thinks that Hama Rules govern the Middle East conflict. They are the rules that Israel has learned to play by. Friedman notes that the former prime minister of Israel, Ariel Sharon, is the one man Assad feared and respected, because Sharon played by those rules too. His support of the Lebanese Falangists in the mass killings at Sabra and Chatila and the recent Israeli reprisals against the Palestinian community are evidence of this. If Friedman's thesis is correct, we in the West are dealing with warriors who are playing by a different set of rules than ourselves. Our notions of proportionate response and the distinction between combatants and noncombatants don't apply to Osama bin Laden, Iman al Zawahiri, and al Qaeda. As bin Laden has announced, every American is an enemy and ought to be destroyed, whether he or she is a soldier or civilian:

> The ruling to kill the Americans and their allies—civilians and military—
> is an individual duty for every Muslim who can do it in any country in
> which it is possible to do it, in order to liberate the Al Aksa Mosque and
> the holy mosque from their grip, and in order for their armies to move out
> of all the lands of Islam, defeated and unable to threaten any Muslim.[9]

During the Cold War, at least we knew that our enemy loved life as much as we and would be motivated by secular self-interest, so that a policy of mutually assured destruction (MAD) was feasible. But now we are confronted by enemies who would just as soon cause a nuclear holocaust that would wipe us and them from the face of the earth, liberating them for heavenly bliss. They play by Hama Rules, with a theocratic touch.

Clash of Cultures

A second characteristic of the recent terrorist attacks is their religious underpinning. Unlike nationalistic terrorist attacks by the IRA, Tamil Tigers, or PLO, these are not done in the name of a nation. They are rooted in culture, namely, a religious worldview and practice, and represent what Samuel Huntington refers to as a "clash of civilizations."[10] The terrorist attacks carried out against the Egyptian government and the al Qaeda–sponsored attacks against the US embassies in East Africa and the World Trade Center and Pentagon were religious in nature. Osama bin Laden, Iman al Zawahiri, and their cohorts have announced that this is a jihad, a holy war against the *kafir*, the infidel, the Evil Empire of the West, and especially the United States. The al Qaeda network sees itself as the vanguard of an Islamic movement, seeking to overthrow American and Western hegemony in the world, and extirpate their influence in the Muslim world, removing American military bases and Western culture from countries like Saudi Arabia, Egypt, and Kuwait. They also reject our devotion to democracy and equal rights for women. Fathers were regularly beaten in public and even killed under the Taliban rule in Afghanistan for sending their daughters to school. The attack on America was intended to provoke a violent American reaction, which in turn would ignite a worldwide Islamic uprising against the West.

This clash of civilizations, pitting the culture of Islamic fundamentalism against a Western culture composed of modernity, secularity, and democracy, has become the new battleground for humankind. With the Cold War over, ideological differences between cultures have reemerged as the source of conflict. Religion is surpassing nationalism as the foremost threat to world peace and stability. Although the majority of Muslims may eschew the terrorists' tactics, there is something in Islamic culture that predisposes it to violence, the idea of jihad, the holy war against the infidel. Saddam Hussein invoked the jihad, appealing to all Muslims to support Iraq against the United States in the Gulf War, and Iran's

Ayatollah Khomeini has called for a holy war against the West, saying that "the struggle against American aggression, greed, plans and policies will be counted as a jihad and anybody who is killed on that path is a martyr."[11] Some of the Muslim schools, madrassas, throughout the Muslim world teach children that the West is evil and that they have a duty to perpetuate the jihad against it. Although many Muslims reject Islamic fundamentalism, instead emphasizing peace, the idea of jihad is an essential part of Islam and fundamentalist forms of Islam are embattled in war wherever it consists of a critical mass that confronts a different culture. In Lebanon, Islam battles Maronite Christians; in Israel, Jews; in Kashmir, Hindus; in Nigeria, Catholic and Protestant Christians; in Somalia and Sudan, evangelical Christians; in Ethiopia, Coptic Christians; in the Baltics and the former Soviet Union, Orthodox Christians; in Pakistan, the small Christian minority; in Indonesia, Timorese Christians; and in Europe and America, Christians, Jews, and secularists. Tolerance toward the "People of the Book" (Jews and Christians) may be officially advocated by the Qur'an, but fundamentalists such as the Wahhabi sect in Saudi Arabia and Pakistan seize upon the notion of the jihad against the *kafir* to override any tendency toward tolerance.

Religion can be a powerful motivating force. Invoking the authority of God and offering the rewards of eternal bliss, it can be an incentive to extreme acts of both virtue and vice. The religious picture of the universe is all embracing and dominates the life of the true believer. It is hard to reason with religious fundamentalists, for they generally hold their faith or religious assumptions to trump what we in the West call *reason*. Reason, for them, always functions as a strategy within the "bounds of religion alone." In many Muslim countries, such as Iran and Saudi Arabia, if one converts to another religion, such as Christianity or Baha'i, one will be executed, as will the agent who is the instrument of conversion.

When Hama Rules are married to religious fundamentalism, the potential for violence—for terrorism—is born.

Causes of Terrorism

Although cultural attitudes, such as religious dogma, may be a significant cause of terrorism, despair or a sense of hopelessness rooted in oppression, ignorance, poverty, and perceived injustice may be the contributing causes—the soil in which fundamentalism can grow and flourish. Often it is those who have been frustrated by the powers that be who strike out against what they perceive as their enemy.[12] Perceived oppression evokes sympathy in the hearts of many, even to the point of excusing or romanticizing violent responses against the "oppressor." Hence, the French existentialist philosopher Jean-Paul Sartre, in defense of the National Liberation Front in Algeria, wrote, "To shoot down a European is to kill two birds with one stone, to destroy an oppressor and the man he oppressed at the same time: there remains a dead man and a free man." Unfortunately for Sartre's analysis, most of the victims of terrorism are unsuspecting, innocent civilians, including children, no more engaged in oppression than a Bedouin sheep herder, a fireman trying to rescue people from a burning building, a woman trying to run a business from the 100th floor of the World Trade Center, or a commuter going to work on the Underground or a bus in London. However, according to the logic of terrorism there is no difference between these people and the commander at Auschwitz who led innocent people to the gas ovens. The attractiveness of terrorism is exacerbated by cultures that encourage violence as a response to perceived harms and wrongs, such as we illustrated above via the Hama Rules. When a religious or political ideology is present, the tendency to resort to terror may be exponentially increased, so that otherwise normal people may resort to extreme measures in the name of religion, believing that by killing people they are serving God, and thereby ensuring themselves eternal bliss.[13]

Peer pressure, religious sanctions, and quasi-military schemes of hierarchical command-obedience cause the terrorist to focus on the importance of the action rather than his own self-interest, enabling him or her to act in ways we would normally consider irrational in the extreme. We are revulsed by terrorism not because terrorists are cowards, but because their misguided courage is directed at violating the most basic human rights of—and even murdering—unsuspecting innocents. In September 2001 CBS's *60 Minutes* produced a documentary directed by Bob Simon on the life of suicide bombers. Young Palestinian men were selected by radical Islamic leaders to be suicide bombers against Israelis. The youths, believing this call to jihad was a sacred honor, were indoctrinated to the point of believing that through the act of fulfilling kamikaze missions they would become holy martyrs and ascend straight to heaven. Videos were often made of their lives, recording their commitment to die for their cause, and sent to their families, who were led to believe that their sons were dying the death of holy martyrs. After such profound commitment, it would be hard for the youth to back out, return home, ring their parents' doorbells, and announce, "Surprise, Mom, I decided that suicide bombing was not in my best interest." Such comprehensive cultural reinforcement of the suicide bomber and terrorist sets this kind of fundamentalism off from our normal sense of prudent and moral behavior. Poverty and oppression are not sufficient or even necessary for terrorism, though they are contributing causes. The overriding impetus is a culture that endorses and reinforces violent responses against certain types of cultures, ideologies, and political systems different from its own.

Terrorism has existed from time immemorial,[14] but with the onset of modern technology—including rapid transport; the bomb; the airplane; and chemical, biological, radiological, and nuclear warfare—the threat to society has been exponentially increased. Furthermore, television and mass communication in general give terrorism widespread publicity. *Publicity is the oxygen of terrorism.* Terrorist acts displayed on worldwide networks like CNN compel our attention, and this point has not been lost on the terrorist leaders. It took just a couple of terrorists bombing a marine barrack in Beirut in 1986, killing 241 servicemen, to cause the withdrawal of American and French forces from Lebanon.

A War on Terrorism

Although terrorism has been endemic in human history, there was something horrific about the suddenness and sheer magnitude of the events of September 11. In one fell swoop our illusion of invulnerability was swept away: America's twin pillars of capitalism were struck down. Nations like Israel had experienced terrorism for decades, but we naively thought ourselves safe. Now we know that no one is immune from unpredictable surprise violence. While we were still reeling from this terrible tragedy, four people, beginning with a man in Florida, died of anthrax exposure and several more people, including NBC's Tom Brokaw and Senate Majority Leader Tom Daschle, received envelopes containing anthrax spores.

A war on terrorism was declared by President Bush, and troops were deployed to areas of the Middle East and Central Asia to destroy terrorist bases. However, mobile terrorists move into the Afghanistan mountains or establish a new base in Iraq, Pakistan, or possibly Saudi Arabia. It will be extremely difficult to defeat sophisticated modern terrorism, for these terrorists have neither a state nor identifiable public buildings or institutions; they operate in small, semiautonomous cells that are difficult to infiltrate. In July 2005, *Times Online* reported "that up to 3,000 British-born or British-based people had passed through Osama Bin-Laden's training camps."[15] Perhaps the answer is to alter the conditions in which terrorism thrives, such as poverty, ignorance, oppression, isolation, and injustice. While no doubt part of an enlightened strategy, this is extremely difficult to accomplish since in this case, the ignorance and oppression are associated with religion, namely, Muslim (Wahhabi) fanaticism, which opposes Western liberal values, including women's rights and tolerance of different lifestyles. The same ideology that opposes secular liberal values gives deep meaning to the lives of the adherents of the terrorist groups. The religion of Allah gives purpose, hope, and a practical guide for action to millions of Muslims, who may live more virtuous, or at least more disciplined, lives than their secular counterparts. It is noteworthy that some of the terrorist leaders say the same thing about contemporary American decadence as American Christian fundamentalists leaders like Jerry Falwell and Pat Robertson, who aver that God permitted this horror of the Day of Ignomity because of our drift into secularism and permissive liberalism. At bottom, this is a struggle between moral secularity and intolerant religious theocracy, between a liberal open society and the Hama Rules of a closed tribal society. It represents a supreme challenge to civilization, one not equaled since the rise of Hitler and Stalin.

Terrorism and Just War Theory

What strikes us as especially heinous about terrorist attacks is the callous disregard for innocent life, the incredible imperviousness to destroying the lives of people who are not warriors. Osama bin Laden's announcement that there is no distinction between a soldier and an ordinary American civilian ("Whoever is a taxpayer in America is a legitimate target") strikes us as the epitome of the immoral use of force, and its originator as a moral cretin. The terrorist fails to grasp the fundamental tenets of *jus in bello*, and so a strong moral presumption opposes it. But even though it is normally unjustified, could there be extreme cases in which terrorism is morally permitted?

Here is where Just War Theory becomes relevant. Our deepest ethical reflections do permit certain types of violent responses to evil under certain conditions. We are permitted (and even enjoined) to defend ourselves against harm by resorting to measured violence. The violence must be not only a last resort and aimed at restoring peace, but also proportionate to morally endorsed goals, doing no more damage than is necessary to accomplish our purposes. It must be delivered in careful ways so as to distinguish between legitimate targets—combatants and their instruments of destruction—and illegitimate targets—noncombatants, civilians not directly involved in the war effort. While there are hard cases for Just War Theory, including firing on innocent shields and struggles in situations of extreme emergency, the kind of horrific violence perpetrated by terrorists against innocent passengers in airplanes and in the World Trade Center is beyond the pale of morally considerable action.

Old-Style and New-Style Terrorism and Civil Rights

Anthony Giddens has distinguished between old-style and new-style terrorism and argues that failure to do so has muddled our thinking.[16] In this section I would like to develop his distinction.

Both old- and new-style terrorism refuse to play by the Western rules of war that distinguish combatants from noncombatants. Terrorists cannot hold their own against the superior firepower of established regimes but must fight in the shadows, using deception, surprise, and even disproportionate violence against their enemy. In this sense terrorism is the weapon of the weak. Both old- and new-style terrorism aim at using violence to strike fear and terror into the heart of the enemy, but there are differences.[17] *Old-style terrorism* is the kind that characterized Europe and Asia for years before 9/11—the IRA; the Basque separatists; the African National Congress; the Stern Gang, Irgun, and Haganah of the 1940s; the early PLO; Algerian rebels; the German Baader-Meinhof Group; and the like. Old-style terrorists put constraints on their violence; for example, the IRA refrained from putting bombs in the London Underground and chose their targets carefully. Traditional terrorism is fundamentally local and concerned with traditional nationalist ideology, seeking to establish a state where it perceives the need for national independence. For example, Sterling Harwood argues that the rebels like Sam Adams used terrorist tactics in the historic Boston Tea Party, invading British ships and dumping barrels of tea into Boston Harbor. *New-style terrorism* is quite different. It is the creation of globalism, the burgeoning economic, cultural, and political interdependence in the modern world. It is largely an Islamic reaction to Western secularism and what Islam perceives as Western decadence and disrespect for Islam. Included in it are such groups as al Qaeda, a loosely connected set of Islamic organizations; Armed Islamic Group (GIA); Islamic Jihad; Hezbollah; Hamas; the Abu Nidal Organization (ANO); World Islamic Front for Jihad Against Jews and Crusaders; and the Palestinian Islamic Jihad Movement (PIJ). In what follows I identify five characteristics that distinguish new-style terrorism from its older counterpart. I am not arguing that none of these newer features were present in the older version, only that taken together, new-style terrorism constitutes a new and more dangerous threat to peace and prosperity. Some groups, like the non-Muslim Tamil Tigers of Sri Lanka, seem to embody features of both types of terrorism. While they have a specific political agenda, they have used suicide bombers to wreak destruction on their enemies, including civilians.

Now let me turn to five differences that set off new-style terrorism from old-style terrorism:

1. New-style terrorism rejects modernity and seeks to destroy it, reconstructing a religious society in its place. Islamic groups like al Qaeda oppose democracy in favor of the *Umma* and sharia, Islamic law. American religious fundamentalists generally accept as their standard the rule of secular law and democracy. It's true that both reject the hedonism and decadence of the West, but Western religious people generally accept the principle of tolerance and civil liberties. Islamist fundamentalists' demands are nonnegotiable. One cannot bargain with such terrorists, for compromise is viewed as apostasy. Whereas we are inclined to divide up the world into liberal democracies and nondemocratic regimes, Islamists

divide up the world into Islamic states and non-Islamic ones. Secular liberal democracy is equivalent to infidelity, which must be replaced by an Islamic theocracy. Because new-style terrorism is driven by religious ideology (jihad), the terrorists are confident that they are doing Allah's will, and so will be rewarded for their "good deeds." In this, Islamic terrorists differ from Timothy McVeigh in his bombing of the Murrah Federal Building in Oklahoma City; McVeigh had a plan to change American society, not to destroy it. Perhaps the nineteenth-century anarchists who detonated a bomb in Chicago's Haymarket Square in 1886 seem like forerunners to new-style terrorism, but those rioters had a specific goal, the eight-hour work day.

2. New-style terrorism uses advanced technology (the Internet, e-mail, cell phones, and airplanes as missiles) in a sophisticated worldwide manner virtually unknown to old-style terrorism. The international terrorist network is, to the best of our knowledge, a loose confederation of organizations held together by common purposes (the destruction of modernity and promotion of Islamic fundamentalism) and the use of modern technology. Such technology promotes efficient communication, which leads to coordinated action and ever-greater destruction. The ingenious attacks of September 11, 2001, were accomplished simply with the use of cell phones, the Internet, and box cutters in the hands of determined and intelligent fanatics.

3. Old-style terrorism had limited aims, such as a separate state for its people. New-style terrorism aims at unlimited destruction. Osama bin Laden called for the death of every American, making no distinction between civilians and combatants.

Our notions of proportionate response and the distinction between combatants and noncombatants don't apply to Osama bin Laden, Iman al Zawahiri, and al Qaeda, or to the leader of the Iraqi terrorists, Abu Musab al-Zarqawi, who regularly directs bombs at Shiite mosques as well as pensioners and children. As bin Laden announced:

> The ruling to kill the Americans and their allies—civilians and military—is an individual duty for every Muslim who can do it in any country in which it is possible to do it, in order to liberate the Al Aksa Mosque and the holy mosque from their grip, and in order

for their armies to move out of all the lands of Islam, defeated and unable to threaten any Muslim.[18]

Ramzi bin al-Shibh describes violence as "the tax" that Muslims must pay "for gaining authority on earth."[19] Other statements issued by al Qaeda speak of a jihad, or war between "the nation of Islam" and the West. The messages seem to be mixed, sometimes sounding like specific grievances, at other times like "a clash of civilizations," of two irreconcilable worldviews. Jessica Stern argues that the call to violence seems directed more at bolstering the self-image of young Muslims than accomplishing any specific political reform.[20]

In his *Imperial Hubris: Why the West Is Losing the War on Terror*, Michael Scheuer argues that bin Laden, unlike many terrorists, is a saintly terrorist, "a combination of Robin Hood and St. Francis of Assisi, an inspiring and devout leader"[21] who has the limited goal of getting the United States to change its policy toward the Muslim world. But when one inquires into the details, we find it means changes such as the complete abandonment of Israel, breaking off all relations with Arab states, and leaving Iraq and Afghanistan—hardly changes that could be made by any American administration.

Whatever the ulterior motives—and they may be very mixed—these new-style terrorists show contempt for innocent human lives. From the murder of nearly 3,000 people on September 11, 2001, to the murder of 191 people in Madrid on March 11, 2004, to the hundreds killed in the blowing up of the Bali hotel in September 2002, to the thousands of people killed in suicide bombings in Iraq and Israel, to the beheading of humanitarian workers like Margaret Hassan and Ken Bigley, and the reporter Daniel Pearl, a purposeful set of murderous acts have been unleashed on all who would exercise their right to live in peace.

In the quotation above, the message is that everyone not with fundamentalist Islam is an enemy who deserves to be killed. In a sense the West has been invaded by a worldview that eschews tolerance and freedom of expression as vices and is willing to murder anyone who even criticizes Islam. The author Salman Rushdie has been under a fatwa for years. After the assassinations of two prominent Dutchmen, the politician Pim Fortuyn in 2002 and the filmmaker Theo van Gogh in 2004, by Islamic extremists in retribution for their criticizing Islam, two members of the Dutch Parliament were forced to live in secret quarters under heavy guard. One of them, Geert Wilders, has been living in a prison cell; the other, Ayaan Hirsi Ali, is confined to a military base. They both have received numerous death threats. What is their crime? They criticized Islamic extremism, namely, the kind of extremism that led to the murders of Fortuyn and van Gogh and which threatens them with assassination. The irony of Western liberal society is that it has to restrict their freedom by hiding away innocent people who exercise their right of free speech, while those who would destroy our freedoms have their freedoms protected, so that they walk the streets of our cities and are allowed ample opportunity to carry out acts of violence.

4. One could count on old-style terrorists to prize their own lives, but new-style terrorists are willing to kill themselves in their mission to destroy infidels and whoever is seen as an enemy. Suicide bombing has become a hallmark of Islamic Jihad, Hezbollah, and al Qaeda. If someone is willing to kill himself or herself in order to kill you, your chances of survival are greatly reduced no matter how many armed guards you have. An al Qaeda operative is reported to have said, "You in the West love life. We love death"—referring to the idea of martyrdom, which guarantees one a splendid reward in heaven. Suicide bombing has been on the rise since the 1990s. In 2005 more than four hundred insurgents blew up themselves in their quest to create chaos in Iraq.

5. The fifth difference is weaponry. Whereas old-style terrorism mainly confined itself to conventional arms, new-style terrorism is willing to resort to weapons of mass destruction—to nuclear, biological, and chemical weapons as well as suicide bombing and any weapon that will kill as many of its enemies as possible. The *New York Times* reported in 2005 that looters, probably connected with terrorists, made off with components for nuclear devices that were transported to weapons storage locations in Baghdad in 2003.[22] In 1987 the Japanese terrorist cult Aum Shinrikyo released the chemical agent sarin in a Tokyo subway, killing twelve people and injuring many more. Other groups are reported as having such weapons. José Padilla, an American citizen, has been held in deten-

tion for more than two years as an "enemy combatant" for planning to set off a "dirty" radiological bomb in the United States. Islamic groups have posted instructions for constructing dirty bombs on the Web. Terrorists who sprayed aerosolized anthrax from vans could kill thousands of people. If they released pneumonic plague into an airport bathroom or sports arena, the pneumonia could spread throughout the city, killing thousands. Chemical and radiological weapons could kill thousands of people, cripple our economy, and make our central cities uninhabitable for years. Radiation from a nuclear bomb could make much of Manhattan, Washington, D.C., or Chicago uninhabitable for decades. A few hundred high-yield (say, one megaton) weapons exploded in a short period could create a "nuclear winter," which could envelop the whole Earth and possibly destroy all civilization, although probably not all humans. Those who did survive might carry disease, including deleterious gene mutations. Airborne fallout, more lethal than neutron radiation, would harm people downwind from a blast.[23] We may pray that terrorists never get their hands on sufficient nuclear devices, but the fact is that they may do so. The point is that weapons of mass destruction are ever more lethal and ever more available to the enemies of Western democracy.

Given these differences, we should conclude that the traditional means of fighting terrorism are insufficient for the present threat. Years ago, an old-style IRA leader said to the British security service, "You might be right 99% of the time, but if you are wrong 1% of the time, we will wreak havoc in your cities." This is even more valid today. We live in a time of crisis when new-style terrorism aims at the destruction of our whole way of life. If we are to defeat new-style terrorism, we must be as vigilant and committed to liberal democracy as these terrorists are to Islamic fundamentalism. We are at war with terrorism, but winning such a war entails taking the necessary steps to defeat our enemy without losing our own souls. We must fight using all the resources at our disposal, intelligently and justly. That means we must find a way to promote our freedoms and spread tolerance, and yet take the necessary steps to curtail the opportunities for terrorism. In addition, this means that we must be willing to modify some of our civil rights, including, in some extreme cases, abridging habeas corpus, in order to defend ourselves from these enemies of all we hold dear. We must learn to live with greater scrutiny of terrorist suspects without resorting to racism or vicious blind retaliation. Here we may well support the UK Labour Party's proposal of detention for suspected terrorists. The Labour Party plan, set forth by Charles Clarke, is for the Home Secretary to have discretion in putting suspected terrorists under house arrest or detention for a limited time until the facts can be sorted out.[24] Used wisely, such a precautionary principle, including the abridgement of civil rights for those who seem to be planning terrorist activities, is a reasonable interim measure while the evidence for terrorism is being considered. The American practices of detention seem to be justified in principle by such reasoning, though we may deplore the abuses at Guantanamo Bay and elsewhere. If issuing universal identification cards will enhance our security, this may also be warranted. Even more important is setting up global intelligence networks, a worldwide enhanced CIA, to monitor and combat terrorists activities.

My thesis of curtailing civil rights in extreme cases is controversial and many people, including those who reviewed an earlier version of this book, strongly disagree with it. In response I would ask, Are civil liberties absolutes or simply objectively valid principles aimed at enhancing the quality of our lives, but which can be overridden under extreme conditions? I think most proponents of civil liberties would opt for the latter. For example, suppose we have evidence that agent A has a biological weapon, which he or she is planning to detonate in a crowded market. Unfortunately, because of the manner in which it was obtained, the evidence is not admissible in a court of law. Wouldn't we want the police to detain A? Perhaps those opposed to the precautionary principle don't believe we are in such a dangerous situation. In that case it is simply a matter of specifying what sort of evidence would convince them that such a dangerous situation is probable, but in principle, they would admit the logic of precautionary principle.[25]

The Moral Response to Terrorism

In responding to terrorism we have a number of converging goals. One salient goal is to honor the nearly three thousand victims of the 9/11 kamikaze attacks and other terrorist attacks. This entails attacking the causes of terrorism, eradicating the moral swamp that breeds the mosquitoes of fanaticism, hatred, and indiscriminate violence. We can also honor the fallen more immediately by punishing those who perpetrate such deeds and the terrorist leaders who train, finance, and motivate the perpetrators to destroy innocent life and property. These two goals are conjoined. In the long term we must create a more just world, one conducive to peace, prosperity, and democracy. But in the short term we must end those regimes and organizations that sponsor and promote terrorism, such as the Taliban, al Qaeda, Hamas, and Islamic Jihad. A measured, carefully executed military operation in Afghanistan, while not a substitute for a more comprehensive long-range political strategy, can support, supplement, and augment the goal of global justice. Let me then outline some short-term and long-term goals in assessing the ethical response to terrorism.

I have already mentioned the fact that Just War Theory would endorse a measured response to the terrorist attack of September 11, aiming to punish and deter terrorists and reduce their threat to our society. That we are building a broad coalition with European, Asian, and Islamic nations in this pursuit is one of the good things resulting from wise handling of the disaster of September 11. Every civilized country has a stake in the battle against terrorism. We should also note, but not develop at length, the need for strategies for self-protection, such as strengthening our homeland counterterrorist policy. Our present policy includes the following four principles:

1. Make no concessions to terrorists and strike no deals.
2. Bring terrorists to justice.
3. Isolate and apply pressure on states that sponsor terrorism, forcing them to change their behavior.
4. Bolster the counterterrorist capabilities of those countries that work with the United States and require assistance.[26]

All this seems responsible and worthy of our national support. In addition, counterterrorism must include cutting off the financial resources of terrorists. Terrorists need a support network, including financial support. By undermining a group's economic ability to wage war, as the United States has recently begun to do, we make terrorist attacks more difficult.[27]

An additional policy that seems entailed by these principles is a more scrutinizing immigration control policy. Several of the September 11 hijackers were here legally, and background checks of others would have caused officials concern. Investigators reported that Mohammed Atta, a known Egyptian terrorist who is thought to have been the mastermind behind the terrorist suicide bombings of September 11, originally entered the United States on a legal visa and, when it expired, was still able to use it to gain entry to the United States just before September 11. No background check was ever done on him. The Immigration and Naturalization Act of 1990 (led by Sen. Ted Kennedy of Massachusetts) forbids denying a visa to foreigners simply because they are members of terrorist organizations. Even though fifteen of the nineteen suicide hijackers were in the United States on legal visas—some of them on student visas—the immigration policy remains unchanged. In January 1999 the US Commission on National Security, cochaired by Colorado senator Gary Hart, warned that our immigration system was lax and warned of coming problems: "America will become increasingly vulnerable to hostile attack on our homeland, and our military superiority will not entirely protect us. Americans will likely die on American soil, possibly in large numbers."[28] "The entire system for monitoring and managing foreign visitors is broken. And why is it we grant visas to students from countries that sponsor terror? After all, we know that terrorists have entered the country on student visas," writes Mark Krikorian, director of the Center for Immigration Studies in Washington, D.C.[29]

A striking case that occurred in Canada is that of the Algerian terrorist Ahmed Ressam, who was apprehended before being able to complete his apparent plan to blow up the Los Angeles International Airport in late 1999. Although Rassem had a forged French passport and a terrorist record, the Canadian immigration authorities (Citizenship and Immigration Canada, CIC) allowed him into the country, where he soon obtained welfare benefits. This kind of immigration laxity violates the state's obligation to protect its citizens from attack by securing its borders from external threats. Granted, this is not easy, for we do not want to exclude visitors or worthy immigrants. Millions of foreigners enter the United States each year, many of whom overstay their visas, but better monitoring of these people is necessary if we are to safeguard our freedom. Many security experts argue that Britain's lax immigration policies are responsible in part for the large number of trained terrorists residing there.

On the other hand, we must work with moderate Muslims to police their own communities, as is occurring in England after the July 7, 2005, transit system bombings. Most Muslims see terrorism as anathema to the Qur'an, which tells us that "[h]e who kills one innocent person kills the whole world." Why has no fatwa been issued by any Islamic leader against Osama bin Laden or Abu Musab al-Zarqawi, who are guilty of violating that principle?

National ID cards may have to be issued in the years to come if this proves the best way to protect our liberty. Authorities would use such IDs to detect illegal aliens, those who have overstayed their visas, and criminals. Such identification, which has become public policy in some European nations, need not curtail our freedom, though it may invade a certain privacy; this may be a price worth paying to preserve our security and liberty.

Long-Term Strategies

Let us now turn to some long-term strategies.

National Service

Some good has already come out of the tragedy of September 11. Our country is united in an almost unprecedented way. Democrats and Republicans are bonding and cooperating to build a more vibrant and secure nation. A similar consensus is occurring in England after the July 7, 2005, London Underground and bus bombings. Young people want to serve their country. In addition to the traditional enlisting in the FBI, CIA, and the military services, we should take this opportunity to develop new opportunities for national and world service for young people. A new model of national conscription seems a plausible option. Each able-bodied youth should be required to serve our nation or the world in some beneficial capacity, such as the military, AmeriCorps, the Domestic Youth Corps, or the Peace Corps. In a 2001 *New York Times* essay, Senators John McCain and Evan Bayh called for the government to institute new service programs to involve youth in civil defense, community service, and international service. In return the government would fund the college education of these young people.[30] Such programs have the virtue of helping young people internalize a moral patriotism and at the same time promote worthy goals such as educating the poor, ministering to the sick and elderly, and serving one's nation and the world. If such programs are appropriately organized and administered, they will not hinder personal autonomy, but instead provide a channel for service. Serving one's country provides a mechanism for expressing one's gratitude for all the benefits membership provides us, creates a mechanism for identifying with the moral goals of the nation, thus internalizing a sense of citizenship, and enables us to help make this a better nation. Though the immediate sphere of service should be one's own country, the circle should be expanded to include the entire world. This leads to the next point, the recognition of a universal morality with universal human rights.

Spreading the Message of a Universal Morality with Universal Human Rights

The moral point of view, whether one takes a consequentialist or deontological perspective, is universalistic, based on rationally approved, impartial principles, recognizing a universal humanity rather than particular groups or persons as the bearers of moral consideration. When seeking to rescue a drowning man we do not ask him, "Are you an American or an Arab?" before seeking to save him. We rescue him because he is a human being. We must come to see all humanity as tied together in a common moral network. If all do not hang together, each will hang alone. Since morality is universalistic, its primary focus must be on the individual, not the nation, race, or religious group. We are all essentially human beings, and only accidentally citizens of the United States, Afghanistan, Germany, Japan, Brazil, or Nigeria. Many of us are grateful to be Americans, but we didn't earn this property, and should recognize that our common humanity overrides specific racial or nationalistic identity. A global perspective must replace nationalism and tribalism as the leitmotif of ethical living. A nonreligious ethic, based on rational reflection and yielding universal human values, must become the underpinning of a renewed cosmopolitanism.

The threats to morality today come from religious particularism, naive egoism, ethical relativism, and deconstructionism—a euphemism for moral nihilism. A defensible moral objectivism, the core of which is accepted by a consensus of moral philosophers, must permeate our society as well as every society under the sun. At present most people derive their moral principles either from religion or from narrow tribal ideology. An educational process inculcating universal norms in people everywhere is a crucial task for the leaders of the twenty-first century. Principles that forbid murder (the unjust killing of innocents), dishonesty, and exploitation and that promote reciprocal cooperation, freedom, and universal justice must be seen as the necessary conditions for the good life, civilization, and peace. I will develop these ideas in my next two chapters. The long-term goal of our war on terrorism leads to the possibility of the establishment of a morally responsible world government. To that subject I now turn.

Notes

1. An earlier version of this chapter appeared in James Sterba, ed., *Terrorism and International Justice* (New York: Oxford University Press, 2003).

2. Quoted in Magnus Ranstorp, "Terrorism in the Name of Religion" *Journal of International Affairs* 50, no. 1 (1996).

3. R. J. Rummel, *Death by Government* (New Brunswick, NJ: Transaction Publishers, 1994). Long before Lord Acton, in the eighteenth century, Edmund Burke wrote, "Power gradually extirpates from the mind every humane and gentle virtue."

4. Howard Sachar, *A History of Israel: From the Rise of Zionism to Our Time* (New York: Knopf, 1996), pp. 267, 333. I do not mean to pick out Israel as worse than the Arab nations or Palestinian leaders. On the contrary, Israel at least approximates a democracy, whereas few of her Arab neighbors, including Saudi Arabia and Egypt, make the slightest pretensions thereof. While Irgun, Etzel, and the Stern Gang were carrying out terrorist acts on Palestinians, Palestinian groups led by such men as Fawzi el-Kutub and Abdul Kader Husseini were blowing up Israelis. We should also include many incidents of America's treatment of the Indians as terrorist acts.

5. A good source for the record of the logic of terror is Alan M. Dershowitz, *Why Terrorism Works* (New Haven, CT: Yale University Press, 2002).

6. Quoted in ibid., p. 15.

7. Thomas Friedman, *From Beirut to Jerusalem* (New York: Farrar, Straus and Giroux, 1989), p. 95.

8. Ibid., p. 89.

9. Osama bin Laden, quoted in Jeffrey Goldberg, "The Education of a Holy Warrior," *New York Times Magazine*, June 25, 2000.

10. See Samuel Huntington's "The Clash of Civilizations?" *Foreign Affairs* 72, no. 3 (1993): 22–50 for an analysis of this phenomenon.

11. Ibid., p. 35. In this regard, Bernard Lewis wrote in 1990, "We are facing a movement far exceeding the level of issues and policies and governments that pursue them. This is no less than a clash of civilizations—perhaps irrational but surely historic reaction of an ancient rival against our Judeo-Christian heritage, our secular present, and the world-wide expansion of both." (Quoted in ibid., p. 32).

12. Some on the political left have blamed globalization for the recent spate of terrorist attacks. David Held of the London School of Economics writes, "In our global age shaped by the flickering images of television and new information systems, the gross inequalities of life chances found in many of the world's regions feed a frenzy of anger, hostility, and resentment. . . . [W]ithout an attempt to anchor globalization in meaningful principles of social justice, there can be no durable solution to the kind of crimes we have just seen" ("Violence and Justice in a Global Age," *openDemocracy*, September 14, 2001, www.opendemocracy.net/conflickt-globaljustice/article_144.jsp). Rooting globalism in principles of social justice surely is called for, but the fact is that the Islamic societies (Afghanistan, Algeria, Iran, Iraq, Libya, Saudi Arabia, Sudan, Syria, and Yemen) that spawn the kind of virulent terrorism we have seen recently are among those that eschew globalism. None of them belong to the World Trade Organization, the pivotal globalist organization. Islamic nations tend to be collectivist and closed societies. Globalism may be a disruptive process, but it fails to explain Islamic extremism because it hasn't touched most of that world. But perhaps it is the *fear* of modernity among Islamic fundamentalists that contributes to violent attacks on the West. See Brink Lindsey, "Why Globalization Didn't Create 9/11," *New Republic* (November 12, 2001).

13. See Salman Rushdie, "Yes, This Is About Islam," *New York Times*, November 2, 2001.

14. The idea of jihad or a holy war of terrorism occurs in the Jewish/Christian Bible. See, for example, the Old Testament book of Exodus (23:23) where God commands the tribes of Israel to blot out all of their neighbors, "the Amonites, and the Hivites, and the Hittites, and the Perizites, and the Canaanaites, the Jebusites," and the book of Joshua, chapter 8, where in the battle for the city of Ai God commands Joshua to kill all of the people in the city.

15. Robert Winnett and David Leppard, "Leaked No. 10 Dossier Reveals Al-Queda's British Recruits," *Times Online* July 10, 2005, http://www.timesonline.co.uk/article/0,,22989-1688872,00.html.

16. See Anthony Giddens' "Terrorism and Civil Rights," *International Herald Tribune*, March 4, 2005, www.iht.com/articles/2005/03/03/news/edlord1.php, which prompted my reflections on this topic.

17. I am not claiming that terrorism is never morally justified, though I believe a very strong prima facie case exists against it.

18. Quoted in Goldberg, "The Education of a Holy Warrior," *New York Times Magazine*, June 15, 2000.

19. Quoted in Jessica Stern, "The Protean Enemy (Al-Qaeda)," *Foreign Affairs* 82, no. 4 (2003).

20. Ibid.

21. Michael Scheuer, *Imperial Hubris: Why the West is Losing the War on Terror* (Washington, D.C.: Brassey's, 2004), p. 19. Scheuer is correct to argue that we must know our enemy if we are to defeat him, but he seems to have mistakenly romanticized bin Laden even as his opponents have exaggerated his evil intentions.

22. James Glanz and William J. Broad, "Looting at Iraqi Weapons Plants Was Systematic, Official Says," *New York Times*, March 13, 2005.

23. I am indebted to the biophysicist John Jagger for a description of the devastation caused by nuclear weapons. See his *The Nuclear Lion* (New York: Plenum, 1991).

24. The House of Lords ruled against the bill on March 7, 2005, but it contains some wise judgments and may be passed in an amended form. The European Union's Commission on Human Rights has already approved a measure allowing terrorist suspects to be held for up to fourteen days until it can be decided whether enough evidence exists to put the suspect on trial.

25. I am grateful to Sterling Harwood, Stephen Kershnar, Max Hocutt, Jim Landesman, Ruth Pojman, Ken King, Peter Tramel, Matt Kramer, John Kleinig, Jonathan Harrison, Mary Gilbertson, and Jim Janes for comments on an earlier version of this chapter. I could not make all the revisions they recommended lest it become larger than intended. In this chapter I am not trying to solve the long-run terrorism problem, but only arguing that new-style terrorism raises the seriousness of the problem so that we have to revise our notions of civil liberties.

26. For a thorough discussion of these principles, see Paul R. Pillar, *Terrorism and U.S. Foreign Policy* (Washington, DC: Brookings Institute Press, 2001).

27. For a cogent analysis of this thesis, see James Adams, *The Financing of Terror: Behind the PLO, IRA, Red Brigades, and M-19 Stand the Paymasters: How the Groups that Are Terrorizing the World Get the Money to Do It* (New York: Simon & Schuster, 1986).

28. Quoted in "Immigration and Terror: The Threat from Enemies Within," *Middle American News*, November 2001.

29. Ibid.

30. John McCain and Evan Bayh, "A New Start for National Service," *New York Times*, November 6, 2001. The two senators plan to introduce legislation in the Senate to effect such a program.

2

The Case for World Government

Ideas of economic and political philosophers both when they are right and when they are wrong are more powerful than is commonly understood. Indeed, the world is ruled by little else. Madmen in authority, who hear voices in the air, are distilling their frenzy from some academic scribbler of a few years back. . . . Sooner or later it is ideas, not vested interests, which are dangerous for good or evil.

—John Maynard Keynes

IN THE FIRST CHAPTER I DESCRIBED the growing menace of nonstate terrorism on people everywhere, from Baghdad (where more civilians are being killed by suicide bombers than by coalition forces), to Istanbul, to Indonesia, to Madrid, London, and New York. Terrorists attack our civilized way of life, rejecting democracy and human rights, especially the rights of women. New-style terrorism rejects the distinction between combatants and civilians, so it will blow up children receiving candy from a soldier. The hallmark of new-style terrorism is the suicide bomber, epitomized in the attacks on the World Trade Center, who is willing to kill him- or herself in order to spread death and chaos. In chapter 1, I said that these attacks of September 11 and those in Indonesia, Madrid, and London were a metaphorical hole of hell; a hole had been blown out of the wall of civilization and, peering through the yawning gap, we were given a glimpse of the barbarism lying on the other side. With this attack a new era in the history of warfare was inaugurated, one that portends a new dimension of evil and a different type of war. The history of the United States will henceforth be divided into Before 9/11 and After 9/11.

For most Americans the terrorist attacks intensified their feelings of patriotism, of national loyalty. Flags appeared out of nowhere on cars, houses, and even on mountaintops. All this seems understandable, but a more complex bivalent reaction may be more fitting. The instinctual patriotic reaction is natural, but the attacks should also cause us to pay greater attention to the rest of the world. If we thought we were impregnable before September 11, 2001, or July 7, 2005, the events of those days should have disabused us of that illusion. The world is becoming an ever-shrinking global village in which events in one neighborhood tend to reverberate far beyond their point of origin, extending to remote parts of the world. Globalism holds much promise. It also brings unwanted consequences, but for good or bad it will not go away, but must be dealt with. What I wish to do in this chapter is set forth the best arguments available for both nationalist commitments and cosmopolitanism, and then try to reconcile them within a larger framework of institutional cosmopolitanism. My thesis is that in an international Hobbesian anarchical world like ours, increasingly threatened by weapons of mass destruction, institutional cosmopolitanism—that is, world government— offers the best prospect for long-term global peace with justice.

Let us define the terms *nationalism* and *cosmopolitanism*. Nationalism designates the thesis that our first loyalty should be to our nation-state. Cosmopolitanism designates the thesis that our first loyalty should be to humanity as a whole. Nationalism is an extension of moral particularity. It is rooted in our intimate relations with family, friends, and community and extends outward to include all those of our political and cultural group. As such it is deep but narrow. It is deep in that it goes to the very heart of our identity and emotional commitments. It is narrow in that it does not expand beyond the primary group or take in the stranger or outsider. Some philosophers hold that moral particularism is the correct moral theory. Universalism is the thesis that a set of moral principles applies impartially to all persons. As such, it appears wider but more shallow than particularism, but universalists can accept that particularism contains a partial truth without adopting it as the central meaning of morality.

The modern institution, the nation-state, begins in Europe with the Peace of Westphalia in 1648, a treaty that marked the end of the Thirty Years' War between Roman Catholics and Protestants, which wreaked havoc through the continent. This settlement stipulated that the religion of each territory was to be determined by the prince of that land. As such, it legitimated a world order in which the major premise was state sovereignty with recognized territorial boundaries, with the minor premise of pluralism, involving mutual respect among members of the international society. The sovereign had sole authority to adjudicate internal matters and declare war. The corollary was that each nation had an obligation of noninterference in the affairs of other sovereign states. The state also had the right to enter into treaties with other sovereign states. Hugo Grotius's work on just war theory, *De Jure Belli ac Pacis* (On the Laws of War and Peace, 1625), the philosophical manifesto of the treaty signed at Westphalia, stipulated that only states have the right to declare war. Grotius developed ides of the earlier Catholic thinkers Augustine, Francisco Suarez, and Francisco de Vitoria, seeking to constrain violence while still recognizing the legitimacy of war as an instrument of national self-determination.

Nationalism became the instrument for uniting ethnically and religiously similar people into a common set of institutions. The movement sought to empower an ethnically or culturally similar people, consolidating them by developing a common set of laws and loyalties, creating a greater degree of autonomy and self-determination. In the nineteenth century the German and Italian provinces were united into nation-states. In Asia, China became a single nation. In the twentieth century nationalism reversed direction and became a source of conflict as people identified themselves according to their ethnic and national assignment, viewing nonnationals as threats and enemies. The worst example of this negative nationalism was German Fascism under the National Socialist Party with its "Ein Volk, ein Reich, ein Führer!" The genocide and "ethnic cleansing" that occurred in the Balkans and Rwanda in the 1990s and Darfur, Sudan, in 2004 are recent testimonies to this dark side of nationalism, often becoming a kind of tribalism. But nationalism in itself is not evil, as I will now argue; it is the promise of morally admirable commitments.

The Promise of Nationalism

For good and for bad, nationalism is a powerful force in the world. Modern nationalism is the quest for self-determinism, for sovereignty, wherein each nation or complex of nations becomes an autonomous political body. David Carment has estimated that there are more than five hundred ethnic minorities in the world, many of them seeking self-determination.[1] These include Chechens in Russia, Uighurs in western China, Basques in northern Spain, Kurds in Iraq, and Palestinians in Israel. The claims of these groups to secession and self-determination vary in their relative merits. Let us consider four generic arguments in favor of nationalism.

The first is the self-determination argument. It is based on the thesis that just as individuals have a right to autonomy, associations of people should be in charge of their own destinies, and groups of people should govern themselves both locally and corporately as much as possible. It is a corollary of our right to be free from external coercion. As noted above, since the Peace of Westphalia Western society has recognized the nation-state as the sole agency of coercion within a territory. Since that time borders have been regarded as sacrosanct, not to be infringed except in a just war of self-defense. The American Founding Fathers justified the war of independence from Britain on the grounds of self-determination. "When in the course of human events, it becomes necessary for one people to dissolve the political bonds which have connected them with another" and assert "separate and equal" status, this is the "right of the people."[2] Just as you and I want to be free to direct our own lives, we want our government to be free from external coercion. This is the quest of the Kurds in Iraq, the Palestinians in Israel, the Chechens in Russia, the Uighurs in Central Asia and China, the Québécois in Canada, and even the native Hawaiians in Hawaii. Perhaps the internecine bloodshed in Bosnia, Kosovo, Israel, Rwanda, and Chechnya could have been avoided if the revolting groups had been given independence. Michael Walzer has argued that justice requires a bounded community in order to make appropriate allocations and that people have a ineluctable tendency to bind themselves together in a common culture and community: "To tear down the walls of the state is not . . . to create a world without walls, but rather to create a thousand petty fortresses."[3] Like clubs and families, they should have some control over who is admitted and who is excluded. This seems correct, but it is not clear just what it establishes.

While self-determination as an extension of autonomy may be a valid goal, this point itself does not establish a justification for an independent nation-state. A further premise is needed to support the idea of a sovereign nation-state. All this argument supports is autonomy, not absolute self-determination. When it violates the human rights of some of its subjects, a nation-state may forfeit its right to self-governance, as Serbia did in its recent policies of ethnic cleansing. A sovereign world government could contain semiautonomous nation-states, just as the sovereign United States of America contains fifty semiautonomous states. This federalist model could be the basis for national enclaves with local self-governance, each containing particular laws, including things like immigration policy and local customs, within a democratic framework, as long as no human rights are violated.

Just what exactly should be the necessary or sufficient conditions for this kind of self-determining nationalism is a difficult question. In the nineteenth century the motto "One people, one state" was interpreted to mean a group with a common culture and ethnic background was naturally suited to self-governance. This motive united the Italian territories into the state of Italy and the Germanic states into the nation of Germany. But in the twentieth century, the motto became the rationale for separating people from their larger states as secessionist movements increased. In a world where the ghosts of past evils still haunt the present, it is probably a reasonable concession to human nature to support some nationalist claims for a separate state. As we countenance a divorce when all attempts at reconciliation have failed, secession from the larger body should be allowed as a last resort. Like the ending of a destructive marriage, secession into a separate national identity may sometimes be the lesser of evils. But it is not something we should celebrate, nor is it free from dangers. Untangling the competing claims of groups within a territory is often a Herculean task. As we learned in India after independence in 1947, when Muslims and Hindus were forced to migrate between Pakistan and India, and, more recently, in Bosnia, where Bosnian Muslims, Croats, and Serbs lived in the same neighborhoods and apartment complexes, great suffering may be caused by uprooting and transferring people from one location to another. Nevertheless, in spite of these qualifications, the right to self-determination has significant merit.

The second argument for nationalism concerns personal identity. Identifying ourselves with a national group seems to give us something that we deeply need: a larger ego, an extended self, a deeper and more

concrete identity. Just as we all value our family, its intimate and pas-
sionate relations defining who we are, we similarly need the sense of belonging that comes via association with larger groups such as our community, our school, our club, our church, our ethnic group, and our
nation. Just as the deep relationships of family—being a child of A and
B, having children C and D, being the brother or sister of E and F—give
profound meaning to our lives, so the nation gives meaning on another,
more abstract but still particular level. In such intimate relations persons are not replaceable the way a doctor or bus driver or shortstop or
car salesman or political leader is. My relationship with my wife consists
in a shared history, memories of our first date in Greenwich Village, our
honeymoon in the Pocono Mountains, hiking together in the Alps and
the Grand Canyon, the birth of our children, those beautiful moments
in exotic places, our struggles and adventures and special joys and sor-
rows. She is not replaceable. Even if cloning were possible, the clone
would not be her. A re-created exact replica of her would not have her
memories or experiences. She is unique. As such, she constitutes a vital
part of my identity. In an analogous manner our relationship with our
community and nation is also irreplaceable, unique and precious, and
constitutes a vital part of our identity.

Some philosophers, like Alasdair MacIntyre, Michael Sandel, Nel
Noddings, Jonathan Dancy, Bernard Williams, and David Miller, go
even further with this feature of our moral repertoire and argue that it
is precisely these particular relations, not the abstract universal principles, that generate our ethics.[4] These philosophers actually reject classic universalist ethics, the idea that ethics consists in universal moral
principles applicable to all people at all times. Instead, they argue that
universalism is too abstract to justify our special obligations to family,
community, and nation. Morality flourishes in concrete relationships
that give meaning and purpose to our lives; we misconstrue the subject when we transform it into the abstract, bloodless universal principles of the core morality.

What are we to make of their argument? Should particularism replace
universalism? The particularist may be conflating the context of discov-
ery with the context of justification. It is no doubt true that we discover
what morality is about through the intimacy of family and communal
interaction, but it is difficult to see how this undermines universalism.
The universalist agrees that we have special obligations to family, friends,

and community, but this obligation is not particular to us, but to all people in all communities everywhere. For example, rule utilitarians argue that we will maximize utility if we concentrate on helping those close to us, our individual families and communities, rather than trying to give equal attention to people in other countries, for we understand our close relations better than we do strangers and foreigners and are more likely to maximize welfare if we concentrate on their needs. Of course we have obligations to people in other countries, but they seldom override our obligations to our families or our fellow countrymen.

We may compare a nation to a team. Take a football team. The members cooperate with one another for a common purpose, to play well and win the game. Each member is concerned to help the other members in a way in which they are not concerned with the good of members of rival teams. They may respect and admire rival team members and refrain from fouls and unnecessary harm, but they aim to win the game, to be the best team in the league, and this requires giving special attention to the needs of fellow teammates consistent with the good of the whole. If a fellow teammate forgets a play or runs a wrong pattern, other members have a duty to correct him; they do not have a duty to correct an opposing player's mistake. Indeed, they hope members of the opposing team will forget plays and run wrong patterns. Conversely, members of other teams have special obligations to their teammates that they do not have to our team. The sports team analogy reminds us that while other nations are rivals and competitors, they need not be enemies. We don't have to treat members of the opposing teams with the same care as we do members of our own team, but they are not enemies. Enemies are perceived as threats to our security and well-being. The danger of the nationalist spirit is to transform competitors into enemies, a game into a war.

Let us return to the thesis that nationhood makes a valuable contribution to personal identity. Traditionally, most nations have been made up of people with a common ethnicity and culture, a single language and history. The genius of the United States of America is that it has been forged out of many cultures and ethnicities into one nation. Immigrants left their countries of origin for the promise of a better life. They left England, Ireland, Germany, Scandinavia, Russia, Poland, Italy, China, Cuba, and Mexico and adopted a new heritage. The many became one people: *E pluribus unum*. While most nations are formed naturally by people living in a common territory and sharing common problems, religion, and language, America is, for the most part, a voluntary nation. New citizens identify with the new culture, not their native one. They learn a new language, adopt new customs, learn to appreciate new literature, identify with a new history, celebrate new holidays—the Fourth of July, Memorial Day, President's Day, the birthday of Martin Luther King Jr.—all significant holidays of their adopted land. And new music like "The Star-Spangled Banner" and folk songs from the pioneer days and the civil rights movement become part of their repertoire. New citizens come to feel the glory of Washington crossing the Delaware to defeat the British, and to agonize over the six-hundred thousand soldiers killed fighting the Civil War, but to be grateful that the war rid the nation of its great evil, chattel slavery. They will take pride in their county's role in the two world wars of the last century and perhaps regret the debacle of the Vietnam War. From the flag to the Fourth of July, from the Statue of Liberty to Silicon Valley, from Wall Street to the White House, new symbols and places will embed themselves in the psyche of new citizens. This is our history. The future of this land is our and our children's future, and so we care for the land, try to preserve its resources and pass them on, as an inestimable patrimony, to new generations. Similar pride and affection characterize all viable nations.

The apex and climax of the nation is the nation-state, the full formalization of the association of people committed to a common purpose. The state imposes institutions onto the people, a governing body, an army to protect them from external harm, and a police force and judicial system to protect them from internal harm and to help them resolve conflicts of interest equitably. It claims sovereignty, to be the sole agent with the right to use coercion within the territory. If the nation represents the substance of the people—their culture, language, rituals, and practices—the state represents the form that gives the substance shape and structure, molding our experience in discrete ways.

Without denying the dark side of nationalism, which often involves hatred of the other and violence and gratuitous suffering, the advocates of nationalism argue that we cannot flourish without its deep psychological benefits. Cosmopolitanism may look good in the abstract but it cannot give humans that particular sense of belonging that the nation affords. It is simply impossible to identify with 6 billion other human beings who live on this planet and with their cultures. We need particular symbols, places, and people with which to identify, which nationalism amply provides. The identity argument may be the strongest arrow in the nationalist's quiver, and the one from which most of us cannot escape.

A third argument enlisted in the defense of nationalism is the argument from self-defense. We need to preserve and protect our culture and our people from harm and destruction. The Israeli writer Amos Oz puts the point most forcefully:

> I think that the nation-state is a tool, an instrument . . . but I am not enamored of this instrument. . . . I would be more than happy to live in a world composed of dozens of civilizations, each developing . . . without any one emerging as a nation state: no flag, no emblem, no passport, no anthem. No nothing. Only spiritual civilizations tied somehow to their lands, without the tools of statehood and without the instruments of war.
>
> But the Jewish people has already staged a long-running one-man show of that sort. The international audience sometimes applauded, sometimes threw stones, and occasionally slaughtered the actor. No one joined us; no one copied the model the Jews were forced to sustain for two thousand years. . . . For me this drama ended with the murder of Europe's Jews by Hitler. And I am forced to take it upon myself to play the "game of nations." With all the tools of statehood. . . . To play the game with an emblem, and a flag, and a passport and an army, and even war, provided that such war is an absolute existential necessity. I accept those rules of the game because existence without the tools of statehood is a matter of mortal danger, but I accept them only up to a point. To take pride in these tools of statehood? To worship these toys? To crow about them? Not I. . . . Nationalism itself is, in my eyes, the curse of mankind.[5]

The nation-state may serve our legitimate interests in that it provides for the protection of our culture and the people associated with it. Of course, as Oz makes eminently clear, this argument is contingent on a world of hostility to one's culture, an anti-Semitic world, in this case. On a smaller scale, the hostility could be localized to an individual state, causing a national group like the Palestinians in Israel, the Kurds in Turkey and Iraq, or the Chechens in Russia to make a claim to secession and an independent state of their own. Conflicts of interest allied with ghosts of the past may haunt our cultural homes so that cooperation and mutual respect become almost impossible. Who is wise enough to adjudicate the historical conflicts between the Protestants and Catholics in Northern Ireland or the Palestinians and Israelis in modern Israel? But one could also imagine a cosmopolitan system wherein forgiveness and reconciliation operated and where prejudice and unjust discrimination were driven underground, if not destroyed altogether. But this world is not the one we live in.

Fourth, there is the multicultural argument for nationalism: The world is a better or more interesting place if it contains diverse cultures. Even if some cultures are correctly judged superior to others, a diverse world is better than a homogeneous one. This is primarily an aesthetic argument: Diversity is interesting, the spice of life. However, it also contains a moral argument: Cultures are experiments in living from which we can learn what succeeds and what does not. By viewing the successes and failures of experiments in living, we can improve our own lives and cultures. However, valid as they are, the aesthetic and moral arguments for cultural diversity do not establish the necessity of the nation-state. Many cultures could exist side by side in the world, just they do in the United States. We could have Italian cosmopolitans, Irish cosmopolitans, African cosmopolitans, Chinese cosmopolitans, and so on. So the multicultural argument does not necessarily support strong nationalism. However, it might support a weaker form of nationalism that serves to protect individual cultures.

To summarize: the arguments from self-determination and personal identity give us strong reasons to promote close community networks. If we include the argument from self-defense and multiculturalism, these four arguments together constitute a cumulative case for nationalism, which justifies the institution of the nation-state. But we have not discovered grounds for strong nationalism wherein the nation-state is endowed with absolute sovereignty. These arguments lead only to limited sovereignty or state autonomy, not complete freedom to do whatever it wishes. We will return to the idea of limited sovereignty, or soft nationalism, but first I turn to a brief history of and the arguments for cosmopolitanism.

The Case for Cosmopolitanism

> Far along the world-wide whisper of the
>   south-wind rushing warm,
> With standards of the peoples plung-
>   ing thro' the thunder-storm;

Till the war-drum throbb'd no longer, and
the battle-flags were furl'd
In the Parliament of man, the Federation
of the world.[6]

For the cosmopolitan idealist, nationalism is just another vicious prejudicial ideology, like racism and sexism. Albert Einstein called it "the measles of mankind," and urged us to get cured. Why prefer your own nation to people elsewhere who are equally human with abilities and needs similar to yours? From the third century B.C.E. an alternative ideal of the world citizen has been a live option for many. The Greek eccentric philosopher Diogenes the Cynic is alleged to have been the first cosmopolitan, calling himself a "world citizen." The Stoics followed his doctrine, becoming the first people to reject the narrow provinciality of particular loyalties and identify as cosmopolitans. But even before the Stoics, the vision of a Peaceable Kingdom was set forth by the Hebrew prophet Isaiah in the sixth century B.C.E.

The wolf shall dwell with the lamb
and the leopard shall lie down with the kid,
and the calf and the lion and the fatling together;
and a little child shall lead them.
The cow and the bear shall feed
their young shall lie down together,
and the lion shall eat straw like the ox.
The suckling child shall play over the hole of the asp,
and the weaned child shall put his hand on the adder's den.
They shall not hunt or destroy
in all my holy mountain;
for the earth shall be full of the knowledge of the Lord
as the waters cover the sea.
[The nations] shall beat their swords into plowshares,
and their spears into pruning hooks;
nation shall not lift up sword against nation,
neither shall they learn war any more.[7]

Later on the early Christians were a type of cosmopolitan, seeing themselves without a specific state but united with all other Christians in a universal brotherhood: "In Christ there is neither Jew nor Greek, neither slave, nor free, neither male nor female, but you are all one in Christ."[8] Every believer is a Christian cosmopolitan, for there is but one king in heaven, God, and no state but the kingdom of God. Race, gender, ethnicity, and class have been annihilated.

A cosmopolitan ideal appears in other religions besides Judaism and Christianity. A minor movement in Islam has advocated a universal caliphate, applying sharia as universal law to all people everywhere. Most recently Hizb ut-Tahir has set forth a program where the caliphate overrides the laws of the nation-state while giving Jews and Christians, though not Hindus, limited autonomy within their territory.

In the early Renaissance, Dante Alighieri wrote *De Monarchia*, arguing for a moral imperialism guaranteeing universal peace. His argument went something like this:

1. Every community must have a ruler.
2. The human race constitutes a single community.
3. Therefore the human race must have a single ruler.

Dante argued that a single disinterested benevolent ruler was required to adjudicate conflicts of interest and apply the law fairly. He claimed that the Roman Empire at its best in its Pax Romana provided such a system.[9]

In the eighteenth century the French thinker Charles Irénée Castel, the Abbé de Saint-Pierre, set forth a proposal for world government, and Immanuel Kant, stopping short of world government, proposed a league of nations consisting of all republican governments and united by a commitment to international law.

In the nineteenth century the Russian count and writer Leo Tolstoy was the foremost cosmopolitan, characterizing patriotism as a kind of corporate insanity. In a little-known essay written in the 1890s, Tolstoy condemned the idea of patriotism as a superstitious and dangerous emotion, tending to produce war and xenophobic behavior that falsely supposes that one's own nation is superior to all others, so that it is always justified in settling grievances violently by use of force.[10] But moral people, especially Christians who follow Christ in his glorification of peace, should eschew such folly, which promises only division, death, and destruction. Instead, they should commit themselves to universal peace and brotherhood. Tolstoy recounted two contemporary celebrations of the Franco-Russian Alliance, one in Kronstadt, Russia, and the other in Toulon, France, both aimed at cementing their alliance and aiming at conducting joint hostile maneuvers against Germany. He commented that such mass hysteria and misplaced loyalty are promoted by the leaders of nations with the assistance of the media and educational system in order to ensure that "cannon fodder," the common people, is available for their future self-aggrandizing adventures. Patriotism, which is nationalism brought to consciousness, is nourished by senseless jingoism in the garden of xenophobia, for it depends on finding an outsider to hate sufficiently so as to enable the people in the in-group to live in peace and cooperate with one another, so long as their hate is directed outward. But a moral conscience must condemn such evil and work for a cosmopolitan outlook, wherein all human life is viewed as sacred.

In the twentieth century the French philosopher Jacques Maritain, the Indian Nobel laureate Rabindranath Tagore, and the American philosopher Mortimer Adler promoted the ideal of world government and citizenship. Maritain argued for the death of the dysfunctional nation-state and the inauguration of world government in which peace and justice will be guaranteed. Given the possibility of nations destroying each other through atomic weapons, an international authority is necessary to ensure peace; the traditional nation-state no longer serves a viable purpose and will have to give up its sovereignty in favor of an international government. Maritain defended his proposal via the idea of a universal natural law, which he believed to be inherent in all human beings and which can be recognized by all rational beings.[11]

Most cosmopolitans in the twenty-first century, like Charles Beitz, Thomas Pogge, Clarence Jones, and Peter Singer, tend to be moral cosmopolitans, aiming at global social justice involving redistribution of wealth, but stopping short of global institutional governance. My proposal supports a global institutional governing body, which in turn will ensure peace and redistribute wealth.

I turn now to a description of a set of events that are vectors, moving us toward globalism and, by extension, the possibility of cosmopolitanism. After this I will discuss the moral arguments for a cosmopolitan attitude and then for institutional cosmopolitanism.

The Power of Globalism

First I want to briefly identify nine global nonmoral forces that are bringing the people of the world into closer contact. They are:

1. Transnational Corporations and the World Market
2. Transportation and Migration
3. Communication
4. Environmental Concerns and Global Warming
5. Health
6. Cultural and Linguistic Forces
7. Unclaimed Geography and Outer Space
8. International Law
9. Peace and Security

Transnational Corporations and the World Market

Imagine a wondrous new machine, strong and supple, a machine that reaps as it destroys. It is huge and mobile, something like the machine of modern agriculture but vastly more complicated and powerful. Think of this awesome machine running over open terrain and ignoring familiar boundaries. It plows across fields and fence rows with a fierce momentum that is exhilarating to behold and also frightening. As it goes, the machine reaps enormous rows of wealth and bounty while it leaves behind great furrows of wreckage.

Now imagine that there are skillful hands on board the machine, but no one is at the wheel. In fact, this machine has no wheel, nor any internal governor to control the speed or direction. It is sustained by its own forward motion, guided mainly by its own appetites. And it is accelerating.

The machine is the subject of this book: modern capitalism driven by the imperatives of global industrial revolution.[12]

Transnational corporations are the leitmotif of globalism, its driving force. If one compares the revenues of the twenty-five largest transnational corporations (TNCs) with the world's top nations, one sees that only six nations have revenues higher than the top TNCs. These companies have assets greater than the gross domestic products (GDP) of most nations. The wealthiest, like Wal-Mart ($246 billion in revenues, 2003),

General Motors, Exxon-Mobil, Royal Dutch Shell, and several automobile manufacturers have assets in the hundreds of billions of dollars, with annual revenues larger than the GDP of all but the wealthiest fifteen or twenty nation-states. General Motors has revenues roughly the same as Ireland, New Zealand, and Hungary combined, larger than Turkey or Denmark; Ford has more than South Africa; Toyota and Exxon, more than Norway or Poland. The revenues of the top five corporations double the GDP of all South Asia.[13] These companies have enormous economic power, and tremendous political potential as well. Exxon has as many ships as the British navy.[14] The TNCs have their own diplomats, called lobbyists, and security forces, which for all intents and purposes are miniature armies. Halliburton and other companies have security forces in Iraq now, virtual armies to help defend their people and property.

These new megacompanies are enormously powerful, decentralized, and interdependent. Flows of US trade and investment are now equivalent to more than 30 percent of the US GDP. In Seattle workers are building the Boeing 777 with parts manufactured in twelve countries. Sixty percent of the Sony workforce is now outside Japan. IBM has begun to lose its American identity. IBM Japan employs eighteen thousand Japanese workers, having become one of Japan's major computer exporters.[15]

Corporations are powerful artificial persons. Unlike real persons, who eventually die, they can go on indefinitely, growing in wealth and power. Although they cannot vote, they can influence and mobilize the votes of thousands. Unlike powerful people in a democracy, corporations are not accountable to a specific state. They are accountable only to their shareholders, who seldom are involved in day-to-day decisions. With their huge legal resources and insurance policies, they are protected from the punishments that would visit private citizens for criminal acts. TNCs can lay off thousands of workers while giving their CEOs billion-dollar raises. They are highly decentralized, irresponsible, mobile, global powers like nothing that has appeared on earth before. The ideal transnational corporation produces products where costs are lowest, sells them in the more affluent markets, and shifts the profits to where tax rates are lower or nonexistent. This ability to move from country to country weakens the bargaining power of the local workers, shifting it decisively to the corporation. The flight of TNCs to places where labor is cheaper may be good economics, but the repercussions on local communities where jobs have been lost is often devastating.

The state is like a tree, essentially immobile. While it can expand its access to resources by extending its roots into the soil in which other trees are growing, it must adapt to its local environment. Like omnivorous animals, corporations are mobile, able to move from tree to tree, taking shelter in the branches, deriving benefits both from the trees, which protect them, and from the other members of the ecosystem, exploiting resources to maximize profits. The exploitation has now become so great that most of the trees in the forest appear to be suffering from what environmentalists call "die-back."[16]

A reaction to globalism is also arising. David Korten likens it to the *Star Trek* episode about the planet Ardana, where the rulers lived in idyllic luxury in the peaceful city of Stratos high above Ardana's desolate surface while down below the inhabitants, the Troglytes, worked in misery and violence in the planet's mines so that the rulers could maintain their luxurious lifestyle. Such is the relation between TNC rulers and their workers.[17] Along these same lines, critics like Susan George argue that globalization "is a shorthand for *de facto* exclusion." It is a mockery of human rights.[18] Organized labor is losing influence over the market and the terms of employment. While the top one hundred corporations had more than $4 trillion in sales in 1997 and accounted for 15 percent of the world's product, alas, they employed fewer than 12 million people while paying their CEOs between two and three hundred times more than the average company employee. Workers' wages are insecure, rising here and falling there, but overall organized labor is losing influence over the market and the terms of employment. Labor is relatively fixed, while capital has wings and flies off to more lucrative fields whenever it finds the labor conditions unsatisfactory. In the United States labor perceives free trade as a threat and has shown resentment at what it perceives as dangerous economic policies and corporate globalism, especially passage of the North American Free Trade Agreement (NAFTA) between the United States, Canada, and Mexico. A coalition of antiglobalists vigorously protested and rioted during the World Trade Organization conferences in Seattle and Toronto in 2000 and 2001, respectively, and in Scotland during the meeting of the G-8 in July 2005. Labor's fears are not altogether unreasonable. TNCs are the brains and brawn of the new world order, designing gargantuan worldwide networks and threatening to replace the nation-state as the dominant force in the global economic revolution.

There is a positive side to the growing increase in international trade. Both sides usually profit from free exchange, and the process itself tends to build mutual trust and cooperation. I once heard of a businessman who asked why Japan wouldn't bomb Pearl Harbor today. When no answer was forthcoming he replied, "Because they own it," referring to the considerable Japanese investment in Hawaii. It is simply irrational to bite the hand that feeds you.

Thomas Friedman has argued that a globalized system of informal relations has replaced the Cold War as the dominant social-economic-political fact of our time. It consists of free-market capitalism, through free trade and international competition producing more efficient and private uses of wealth. Individuals, corporations, and nation-states are able "to reach around the world farther, faster, deeper and cheaper than ever before, and in a way that is also producing a powerful backlash from those brutalized or left behind by this new system."[19] Globalization is occurring in virtually every country in the world. Unlike the great nations and empires of the past, this supernational organization has no geographical capital, no center of power. No one nation or corporation can control it. Rapid change, technological advances, and corporate tentacles, spreading into every part of the world, are also creating greater distances between the older, more atavistic or primitive cultures and the new ones budding in their midst. Friedman describes an automobile assembly plant outside of Tokyo where 310 robots, supervised by a few human beings, are building the "world's greatest luxury car, the Lexus." While witnessing this technological miracle, he received a report on his cell phone from Jerusalem, where Palestinians and Jews are fighting over who owns which olive tree. "It struck me," he writes, "that the Lexus and the olive tree were actually pretty good symbols of this post–Cold War era: half the world seemed to be emerging from the Cold War intent on building a better Lexus, dedicated to modernizing, streamlining, and privatizing their economies in order to thrive in the system of globalization, and half the world—sometimes half of the same country—was still caught up in the fight over who owns which olive tree."[20]

Rapidly expanding, fluid, penetrating each segment of the globe, globalization is ushering in a new democratic revolution. The symbol of the Cold War system was the Berlin Wall, which divided everyone. The symbol of the global system is the World Wide Web, which unites more and more people every year. But Friedman may underestimate the disruption in national and traditional economies. Globalism involves tradeoffs, and as such requires supervision, if the pluses are to outweigh the negatives. For good and bad, globalism, with its mobile TNCs, is a vector pointing toward the need for greater realization of international cooperation and understanding, moving us toward the possibility of the cosmopolitan vision. Today these TNCs are like greedy Titans who need to be democratized and subjected to the constraints of international law. A global governor is required to prevent exploitation of workers, enforce contracts, and promote fair trade, so that indigenous economies can compete in the global market.

Transportation and Migration

Global economics exacerbates the flow of migration, as the poor and upwardly mobile of the world gravitate to places where jobs and better welfare conditions exist. There are about 175 million immigrants in the world and another 150 million migrants are on the move every day, with at least 4 million permanent refugees occupying refugee camps. Many simply trek long distances from one country to another, while others pay often exorbitant sums to "coyotes" and truckers to smuggle them over borders. Some are fleeing war and persecution, others seeking employment and opportunity. Still others arrive as students or tourists and remain as illegal aliens. Regular travel to and fro between nations is common, especially for those with dual citizenship. Rapid, inexpensive transportation makes travel easier and brings us closer together, whether we like it or not. The result is often cultural uprootedness and confrontation between new arrivals and the local community. Virtually every nation in the world is experiencing a whirlpool of multiculturalism. More nations are recognizing the right to dual citizenship. The present International Organization for Migration and the UN refugee agency UNHCR will need more extensive powers to monitor and coordinate refugee and migratory issues in the future.

Communication

The information revolution has broken down the partitions separating one people from another and is providing a highway of communication virtually undreamed of only a half century ago. The Internet and the media have transformed our lives and created a worldwide communication network. Even the terrorists who despise decadent Western values make use of the Web to communicate with one another across oceans. The media aid in spreading news of terrorist incidents and often inadvertently provide the oxygen terrorism needs to breathe. Chinese scholars have reported that such American crime dramas as *Starsky and Hutch* were having an influence on the Chinese public. Taking their cue from these programs, criminals have announced to the authorities their "right to remain silent."[21] Thanks to the Internet, computer analysts in India, South Korea, and Taiwan can read the same advertisement for high-paying IT jobs in Silicon Valley as any American—and apply for them. The main point is that modern communications media are shrinking the globe. A growing international consciousness is manifesting itself as CNN and other news networks beam the latest Asian uprising or African coup into our living rooms, sometimes before the local government is aware of it. The media and World Wide Web may be the most powerful forces contributing to building a worldwide community, breaking down barriers of ignorance and misinformation, and spreading a more homogenized culture.

Environmental Concerns and Global Warming

The world's resources are finite, and the moral point of view requires that we preserve as much of these resources for posterity as possible without unduly sacrificing our own welfare. An incredible number of species are being lost at an alarming rate. The world's rain forests are virtually irreplaceable assets threatened by short-term economic interests. Within the rain forest is a treasure of biodiversity, vital for the production of medicine and food, which is becoming a casualty of our immediate economic policies. The loss of genetic information may never be recovered.

With a growing population eager to reach a Western-style living standard comes increased pollution. Air and water pollution tend to spread, impervious to political boundaries. For example, contaminated air from the nuclear explosion at Chernobyl wafted westward to Sweden, France, Italy, and Switzerland. An increasingly depleted ozone layer over the Antarctic makes all people vulnerable to cancer-causing ultraviolet radiation. Air pollution in the American Northeast has been traced to Chinese coal burning power plants.

One global issue that affects us all is that of global warming. In 1988 Dr. James Hansen, director of the National Aeronautics and Space Administration (NASA) presented evidence of significant global warming, and by current trends the polar ice caps and glaciers will gradually melt, causing the ocean's level to rise several feet. People living on islands and along coastlines would be displaced as their lands became deluged by the sea. The temperate zones would become warmer so that forest fires would be more frequent. Wind and rain patterns would be altered, producing droughts in historically fertile areas. Since Hansen's report was released, climate models have projected that the surface temperature of the earth will rise 2°F to 6°F, with global sea levels rising by six to thirty-seven inches (fifteen to forty-eight centimeters) between 1990 and 2100. The agricultural lowlands and deltas in parts of Bangladesh, India, and China would be devastated, and many Carribean islands would be deluged, as would be the coastal areas of the United States, including Los Angeles, San Francisco, Long Island, and the Carolina coasts. Ocean salt water would contaminate coastal aquifers, and rising sea levels could flood sewage and sanitation systems, spreading infectious diseases. Hurricanes, typhoons, tornadoes, tsunamis, and inland flooding would increase in power and frequency.

On the other hand, ironically, the greenhouse effect could result in a devastating mini Ice Age in Europe. If the North Atlantic ice caps melt, they would send an incursion of fresh cold water into the "conveyor belt" of warm salt water, the Gulf Stream, that is responsible for Europe's temperate climate, thus making northern Europe a frigid zone like northern Canada. Although over 95 percent of climatologists agree that human-created greenhouse gases are likely to cause the kinds of effects just described, skeptics exist who question some aspects of the greenhouse effect thesis. Even if room for doubt exists, the precautionary principle (better be safe than sorry) requires that we modify our lifestyles, cutting back on our use of greenhouse gases like carbon dioxide. In 1997 the Kyoto Protocol set targets for thirty-nine developed nations to cut their greenhouse gas emissions by 2012, aiming to cut back 5 percent below 1990 levels. While most nations signed the Kyoto Accord in 1998, the United States refused. Instead it reached an all-time high of 1.9 billion metric tons of carbon emissions in 2000. The fact that the greenhouse effect is a global problem, calling for universal compliance, in which one nation can flout a global consensus with impunity highlights the need for an authoritative global body to enforce international law. A central environmental agency, such as a global Environmental Protection Agency, will be required to coordinate resource use, protect the rain forests, and enforce regulations on pollution and the use of greenhouse gases. As Thomas Hobbes wrote in 1651, "Covenants without swords are just words."[22] Mutually agreed-upon, mutually constraining regulations are necessary to protect the environment, which in turn is necessary for the protection of our health, a subject to which we now turn.

Health

We are all intertwined in an interdependent global web in other ways as well. A German businessman making a deal in Pakistan picks up a virus that originated somewhere in Africa. He gets on a plane for Frankfurt, infecting the entire planeload of passengers, who spread the disease throughout Europe. An infected American tourist brings the virus with her on a flight from Frankfurt to the United States, where the virus spreads across the country. HIV, the virus that causes AIDS, apparently originated in West Africa, spread to the West, then made its way to Asia and back to East Africa, decimating the populations of Zimbabwe and South Africa and leaving millions of children orphans. The AIDS pandemic threatens millions, especially in Asia and Africa, where 28 million of the world's 40 million cases are found. The Ebola virus caused an epidemic in the Congo and made its way to the primate center in Reston, Virginia, disrupting work and resulting in the death of more than four hundred monkeys; the virus could reappear with even more devastating effects. The coronavirus that causes SARS, originating in China, spread widely throughout the world, infecting more than seven thousand people and killing more than seven hundred, once again illustrating that no country can isolate itself from the misery of other people. The World Health Organization will need additional support from the world community if it is to adequately monitor the spread of disease and coordinate regional and local health agencies in their task of controlling disease.

Cultural and Linguistic Forces

Culture via market exchange is bringing us closer together. Consider the following:

There was once an Englishman who worked in the London office of a multinational corporation based in the United States. He drove home one evening in his Japanese car. His wife, who worked in a firm which imported German kitchen equipment, was already at home. Her small Italian car was often quicker through the traffic. After a meal which included New Zealand lamb, California carrots, Mexican honey, French cheese and Spanish wine, they settled down to watch a programme on their television set, which had been made in Finland. The programme was a retrospective celebration of the war to recapture the Falkland Islands. As they watched it they felt warmly patriotic and very proud to be British.[23]

Becoming tenaciously interdependent, we partake of food, music, electronic equipment, clothes, and commodities from all over the world.

English is becoming the lingua franca of the modern world in the way Greek was in the ancient world. English is now almost universal in science, permitting all scientists in the world to communicate effectively.[24] Western and Eastern music and art are cross-fertilizing each other. Hindu and Buddhist missionaries from India and Tibet are as influential in the West as Christian missionaries from the West once were in the East. The Dalai Lama is one of the most revered people in the West. Literature and film from all parts of the world inform our lives in ways undreamed of only a few generations ago. A historical irony is exemplified in the fact that in order to get to the Museum of Communism in Prague, one must pass the Café Monica (named after Lewinsky), push through the crowds of the McDonald's next door and go through the entrance of a Las Vegas–style casino. What must Marx be feeling now? A Western sexual culture is spreading throughout the world, as Fiji girls try to emulate stars of *Baywatch*, a more promiscuous *Playboy* culture displaces traditional notions of chastity, and CNN broadcasts images of a tearful Monica Lewinsky to remote corners of the world.[25] Monica, MTV, Macintosh, and McDonalds are mesmerizing the developing world with their fast music, fast computers, and fast food. This is the shallow McWorld whose centripetal force into the black hole of nihilism rivals the centrifugal forces of terrorism and war that threaten to unravel the fragile web of international cooperation and destroy civilization.[26] The challenge of our age will be to create a moral consensus that steers safely between the Charybdis of Western hedonism and the Scylla of fundamentalist tribalism. Cultural diversity within broad moral limits of basic human rights is a precious treasure we want to preserve even as we learn to respect each other more deeply. Moral integrity and international law based on basic human rights can be the glue that binds culturally diverse people together.

Unclaimed Geography and Outer Space

A need exists to regulate geographical areas like Antartica, the oceans, and places in outer space, such as the moon or Mars, which humans may reach by space travel. These locations require monitoring for environmental reasons in order to prevent spreading the tragedy of the commons.[27] Places in outer space will require governance once they are seen as having value to humans. It may even be the case that space travel must be regulated lest rockets and other space vehicles become a problem. One can imagine future human beings deciding to get rid of harmful chemical and nuclear waste by sending it off into space—with the danger of the spacecraft blowing up and the waste polluting the earth.

An outer-space agency is required for two purposes: (1) to ensure that outer space is used for peaceful purposes only, and (2) to promote full exploration of outer space for the common benefit of humanity. This includes the development of new rockets and satellites, and the supervision of both manned and unmanned space vehicles and travel.

International Law

International law already exists. Laws regulating diplomacy are quite old, being traced at least back to the Congress of Vienna in 1815 at the end of the Napoleonic Wars. Such laws ensure diplomatic immunity from arrest and search. A nation's embassy is also given such immunity. The Geneva Convention on Prisoners of War of 1929 mandates that prisoners of war be treated humanely and given the same nutrition as the capturing nation's military. The Hague Gas Declaration of 1899 prohibits the use of "asphyxiating and deleterious gases"; a nation may not poison enemy soldiers on the field of battle or elsewhere with noxious gases.

Most international law is created through treaties. Some of these are:

- Partial Test Ban Treaty of 1963, which prohibits nuclear tests in the atmosphere, above the atmosphere and under water.
- Nuclear Non-proliferation Treaty of 1968, which prohibits countries possessing nuclear weapons from giving them to countries without such weapons.
- Biological Weapons Treaty of 1972, which prohibits the production or use of biological warfare.
- Environmental Modification Treaty of 1977, which prohibits tampering with the natural environment for military advantage.

These are all important treaties having global consequences. They are worthy of support. Because of the endorsement of the United Nations Security Council and its corresponding sanctions, some international laws are obeyed. But many others are not. The Kyoto Accord was rejected by the United States because it was deemed harmful and unfair to its economy (China and India were exempt from its regulations). The trouble is, such laws have no teeth. The Hague Gas Declaration of 1899 was violated without penalties by the Germans in World War I and by the Iraqis in their war against Iran in the 1980s. The law granting embassies immunity from attack was violated by the Iranian revolutionaries in November 1979 when they seized the U.S. Embassy in Tehran, holding over one hundred embassy personnel hostage for more than a year. Such a flagrant violation of the oldest international law was justified by the revolutionaries as an attack on US imperialism and espionage. The governments of Pakistan and Libya supported the revolutionaries, claiming that such a law was biased in favor of the Western imperialist powers.

Witness Article X of the Nuclear Non-proliferation Treaty of 1968:

> Each party shall in exercising sovereignty have the right to withdraw from the Treaty if it decides that extraordinary events, related to the subject matter of the Treaty, have jeopardized the supreme interests of the country.

That means whenever a country doesn't like the implications of the treaty, it may violate it with impunity. What kind of law can be broken whenever it is inconvenient?

Law is a conservative instrument sealing in the status quo so that it becomes difficult to change it. Suppose I don't like the laws requiring me to pay income tax. In order to change them, I must engage in a long, difficult political process that is likely to fail, but meanwhile I must still pay my taxes on pain of being arrested, tried, and being put in prison for a number of years.

This domestic legal process contains five components:

1. We have a legislative body to make laws.
2. We have an executive body to supervise laws.
3. We have a police force to arrest violators.
4. We have a judicial system to try the accused.
5. We have a prison system to incarcerate those found guilty.

A viable legal system requires all five components. We have none of these on an international level. The closest we come to them are treaties that are voluntarily signed by the leaders of nations but which may be broken whenever it is convenient. But a law without enforcement is really not a law, but merely an ideal. What we need is an international system of law as follows:

1. A legislative body to make laws.
2. An executive body to supervise laws.
3. A police force to arrest violators.
4. A judicial system to try the accused.
5. A prison system to incarcerate those found guilty.

Such a cosmopolitan system will become necessary as we attempt to deal effectively with international crime. Crime is increasingly becoming international. In our global economy, the United States is increasingly affected by crime originating in other countries. Almost 40 percent of the cases handled by the FBI today, from telemarketing fraud to car theft to drugs and money laundering, crime has international dimensions.[28]

A universal set of laws with fixed penalties that is impartially enforced by a central policelike agency could be a catalyst for security, peace, the protection of human rights, and environmental wholeness. The International Criminal Court (ICC) in The Hague was established in 1948 to try cases of gross human rights violations, such as genocide and state torture. Its sister institution, the Ad Hoc Criminal Tribunal for the Former Yugoslavia (ICTFY), established in 1996, is currently trying the former Serbian leader Slobodan Milosevic, accused of genocide, but neither the ICC or the ICTFY has power to apprehend those accused of crimes, and its power to punish them if convicted is limited. Six nations have offered to imprison those convicted of war crimes. An international Central Intelligence Agency and Supreme Court seem to be needed to handle growing number of human rights violations and international crimes, including terrorist attacks. The gradual recognition of universal human rights that has taken place in the last twenty years is a promising omen of international cooperation in the pursuit of justice and security. In particular, the ICC is a promising development, announcing the message that political leaders will be held accountable for human rights abuses. An international police force is required to apprehend those who commit international crimes and human rights violations, and a global prison system is needed in which to incarcerate them. Whatever the prospects for world government, an international legal institution with a universal body of laws responsive to a universal set of rights will most likely be needed to coordinate behavior and conflicts of interest in the future.

Peace and Security

This last point leads to the topic of terrorism and the need for peace, a main concern of this book. Since the terrorist attacks of September 11, 2001, the United States has had to rely on allies in Europe, especially England and France; the Middle East; and Asia, especially Pakistan, India, and Indonesia, to arrest, deport, and try suspected terrorists. However, the war against terror will be won only when there is universal cooperation in combating it. Furthermore, the threat of the employment of weapons of mass destruction calls for a permanent international monitoring commission.

States are roughly analogous to individuals in a Hobbesian state of nature, where "life is solitary, poor, nasty, brutish, and short . . . a war of all against all." Given nuclear weapons and other weapons of mass destruction, ever more available to smaller nations (like North Korea, Israel, Iran, and Pakistan) and terrorist groups (like al Qaeda), the possibility for these groups and rogue nations to inflict enormous damage on mighty superpowers and the rest of humanity is growing exponentially. The world is becoming a more dangerous place. Just as individuals give up some liberty to the commonwealth in order to attain peace and security, the nations of the world may need to give up a degree of sovereignty in order to attain peace, security, and justice in a world in which we interact in ever-closer ways. The advantages of a world government are (1) having a central agency to maintain the peace, adjudicating between rival claims; (2) having a standing army and a police force to enforce the peace; (3) having a central agency to construct and enforce international law, including devising environmental regulations necessary for health; and (4) having a central agency to collect taxes and redistribute wealth to where it will do most good, ameliorating some of the conditions for terrorism. Ideally, present nation-states within a world federation would be analogous to the fifty states within the United States of America, possessing local autonomy but not absolute sovereignty. From a moral point of view there is nothing sacred about nations. If they serve humanity best, fine. Then they are justified. But if a better, more just arrangement comes along we should adopt it.

Let us now compare two kinds of peace: *negative peace* and *positive peace.*

Negative peace is a state of nonviolence but with the possible threat of war. This is merely the absence of military action between countries, the anarchistic state of affairs existing between most sovereign nations in the world, but especially in such cases as between India and Pakistan, Taiwan and China, North and South Korea, and as was the case between the United States and Iraq before the U.S. invasion of Iraq in 2003. It characterized the Cold War between the United States and the USSR before 1989. Hobbes referred to this latent state of war, writing, "War consists not in battle only, or the act of fighting: but in a tract of time, wherein the will to contend by battle is sufficiently known; and therefore the notion of time, is to be considered in the nature of war; as it is in the nature of weather. For as the nature of foul weather lies not in a shower of two of rain; but in an inclination thereto of many days together; so the nature of war consists not in actual fighting; but in the known disposition thereto, during all the time there is no assurance to the contrary. All other time is Peace."[29]

Positive peace, or civil peace, occurs where mechanisms exist for resolving conflicts of interest via negotiations or law. Such mechanisms exist between the nations in the European Union, and in the United

States between the various states. Positive peace is absent in most of the world where, at best, negative peace exists, such as between India and Pakistan over Kashmir. Cicero wrote, "There are two ways of settling disputed questions: one by discussion, the other by force. The first being characterized by man, the second of brutes. We should have recourse to the latter only if the former fails."[30] And John Locke wrote, "there are two sorts of contests among men, the one managed by law, the other by force; and these are of such nature that where the one ends, the other always begins."[31]

In order to have lasting peace we need to arrive at positive peace, which peace in our day requires an effectively managed legal structure. But an effective universal legal structure requires an authoritative, universally accepted government, such as a world government. It requires that individual states relinquish external sovereignty to a world governing body, which becomes the sole adjudicator of international disputes.

In sum: peace is the long-term goal of all people of goodwill. If war is to be abolished, there must be a mechanism for resolving international conflicts of interests. This points to the need for a central international agency to adjudicate disputes and intervene where violence threatens human rights.

These nine forces are forcing us to think globally, whether we want to or not. Distances between nations and peoples are shrinking. We're becoming interdependent in ways hardly dreamed of in earlier times. We are already becoming one world, whether we choose to do so or not. Our neighbor's problem tends, more often than not, to become our problem. We need to learn to coordinate our resources for mutual assistance. We need enforceable international law to help regulate our behavior. All of this points toward institutional cosmopolitanism. Let us now look at some moral arguments for an internationalist perspective.

Moral Arguments for Cosmopolitanism

I will offer two moral arguments for cosmopolitanism:

1. The Moral Point of View: The Principle of Humanity and the Moral Equality of Persons
2. The Argument from Equal Opportunity

The Moral Point of View: The Principle of Humanity and the Moral Equality of Persons

The attraction of cosmopolitanism is that it seems to embody the heart of the moral point of view, impartially applying moral principles to all humans. When you see a child drowning, you do not first ask her nationality or religious affiliation before rescuing her. You save her because she is a human being. Each human being (more accurately, every person, for this would apply to rational beings from outer space should they turn up and it may apply to higher animals)[32] should have his or her needs and interests taken into consideration and be treated according to his or her individual desert or needs, not according to accidental features, such as one's race, ethnicity, or religion. If there is a universal morality applying to all people everywhere and which can be realized in each human life, one joining us each and all in a common moral brotherhood, then why get sidetracked by the fetish of particular bureaucratic states? Nations with their boundaries are not fundamental features of morality, but at best contingent artificial institutions that are justified only if they serve the human good. To paraphrase Jesus when he broke the Sabbath to serve people's need, "Governments were made for man, not man for government." States are only contingent instruments in the moral repertoire. If they serve human interests, well and good. But if and when we can find a better way to serve human need, we should replace nation-states with it. Kant draws attention to this point when he sets forth his principle of the Kingdom of Ends: All rational beings should be treated as "ends in themselves and not merely as means." All human beings possess a dignity that may not morally be violated by manipulative or coercive behavior (except to prevent a greater injustice). Karl Marx and Friedrich Engels subscribed to the same basic ideal, however naively, when they prophesied that in the ideal communist utopia, the state would "wither away" and humans, overcoming the alienation of exploitative relations, would live in an anarchistic utopia, much like that described by the prophet Isaiah and advocated by Kant. Utilitarians have a similar goal of maximizing welfare and minimizing suffering. All of these moral/political philosophies unite in the goal of promoting universal peace; an end to war, militarism, and state violence; and the end of the bipolar "us against them." Instead we would live in a world where "each contributed according to his or her ability and received according to his or her need," a world of peace, prosperity, and global justice.

The philosophical justification for the principle of humanity is rooted in our common human nature. We are all roughly similar in native ability to reason and suffer and can interact rationally with one another. Morality has to do with promoting human flourishing and ameliorating suffering, and this latter strategy should extend to nonhuman animals.[33] Stoics, Kantians, Marxists, utilitarians, and secular cosmopolitans all seek to implement the universal moral order in a nonreligious manner, creating a secular equivalent to the kingdom of heaven on earth. If we all lived decent moral lives, as brothers and sisters, we would need neither the state nor its army, nor its police force nor its lawyers. It seems so simple, but of course it isn't. Human nature is ambiguous and very complicated, so that utopian community of peace and plenty will continue to remain a long-term goal. We will probably always need law and government to enforce the law. But we would come closer to universal peace and justice if we all become world citizens instead of merely Americans, Russians, Mexicans, Canadians, British, French, or Chinese. Let us turn to the second argument for cosmopolitan justice.

The Argument from Equal Opportunity

The moral point of view presumes moral equality—not equality of results, but equality of opportunity. Justice requires attempting to provide each person with equal opportunity to live a worthwhile life. Every person has a prima facie right to the conditions that would enable one to develop his or her potential to a reasonable degree. This is usually taken to mean "to provide each citizen within a nation with that opportunity." This is true, but why confine this principle to nation-states? Should we not extend the principle to include every human being throughout the world and those yet to be born? We generally believe that it is unjust for someone to have fewer opportunities to develop their lives because of morally irrelevant traits, such as race, ethnicity, cultural identity, religion, or gender. If so, is there any reason we should not add *nationality* to the list of morally irrelevant characteristics? If one goal of morality is to promote each person's flourishing, should we not transcend national boundaries and seek to apply the principle of equal opportunity to all people everywhere? Perhaps the main reason for our failure to do so has to do with our lack of moral imagination. Granted, it would be a prima facie duty, with a correlative right, able to be overridden by other duties or prevented from being realized by recalcitrant social conditions such as where an indigenous culture is antidemocratic and oppressive and cannot be changed without high costs. But the principle of equal opportunity would remain part of our moral repertoire and, as such, guide public policy. We are all human beings, and only accidentally citizens of the United States, Afghanistan, Germany, Japan, Brazil, Rwanda, or Nigeria. Many of us are grateful to be Americans, but we didn't earn this land or the resources within it. We are simply the beneficiaries of the natural lottery. As such we cannot take pride in our land as an accomplishment, as we can over the home we built, the race we won, or grade we received for our philosophy paper. Similarly, while we cannot take credit for the beautiful land and rich resources America offers, we may take pride in what we have done with the land and resources. We have been entrusted with this land and ought to tend it as good stewards for the benefit not only of ourselves, but also of those who will come after us and for those in great need. Regarding natural resources, we should recognize that our common humanity has a claim on us that may override specific racial, nationalistic identity. A global perspective ought to replace nationalism and tribalism as the leitmotif of ethical living. A rational ethic, based universal human values, must become the underpinning of a renewed cosmopolitanism. If this argument is sound, justice, at least in a world of affluence such as ours, creates a prima facie right to equal opportunity, including the right to the basic conditions for living a worthwhile life, such as adequate nutrition, minimal health care, and security.

In this regard, the recognition of universal human rights, which commenced after World War II with the UN Declaration of Universal Human Rights in 1948, is perhaps the most significant achievement of the past fifty years. Shocked by the atrocities of the Nazi and Japanese regimes, the members of the fledgling United Nations set forth a list of basic human rights centered around "life, liberty and security of person," and also "the right to a standard of living adequate for the health and well-being of himself and of his family." These rights and freedoms are universal, applying to all human beings everywhere regardless of race, color, sex, or national or social origin (Art. 2). They include the usual "rights to life and liberty," but add such economic rights as "the right to work" and "the right of equal pay for equal work" (Art. 23), and such welfare rights as "social security" (Art. 23) and a decent standard of living (Art. 25). In sum, the Declaration of Universal Human Rights, while not a perfect philosophical document, embodies the basic principles of objective morality as we have outlined them in the sections on the principle of humanity and the argument from equal opportunity.

At the time these "rights" were seen as little more than a wish list for idealists who were reacting to the horrors of the six-year global war. But in the last twenty years they have taken on some relevance and urgency as the nations of the world have been prompted by these principles to intervene in Serbia-Bosnia, Kosovo, Somalia, and Iraq in order to curtail genocide and the oppression of minorities. While the world failed to intervene in Rwanda, Darfur, and Cambodia, it was left with a sense of guilt that it could have done something to prevent the massacre of millions of innocent lives. Similarly the human rights rhetoric has inspired the moral leadership of Nelson Mandela, against all odds, to bring down the apartheid policy in South Africa and Chinese students to stand up to tanks in Tiananmen Square in 1989. The ideals of human rights inspired the Russians to overthrow the Communist rule in the former Soviet Union in 1991, and the Germans to tear down the Berlin Wall in 1989. Similarly, it has inspired humanitarian agencies like Oxfam, Friends World Service, Doctors Without Borders, and World Vision to assist poor people in the underdeveloped world to have access to minimal health care and education. The Bill and Milinda Gates Foundation has called public attention to its increased committment to the cause of global health care.[34] There is also a growing consensus that political leaders responsible for crimes violating human rights should be prosecuted by an impartial world court. An international court in The Hague was established in the late 1990s and the former Yugoslav dictator Slobodan Milosevic and other accused war criminals are presently being tried by its judges. Attempts have been made to try the former Iraqi president Saddam Hussein by an international tribunal, but the new Iraqi government took over that job. While still in its formative stage fundamentally, global justice today can be equated with the promotion of the broad human rights described in the UN Declaration of 1948. Although progress in realizing basic human rights is slow and uneven, it promises to break down artificial barriers of national boundaries, bureaucratic administration, and the whole post-Westphalian apparatus of the nation-state, bringing all humanity together under a common cosmopolitan allegiance. For this, a comprehensive world government with the power and authority to promote peace, resolve conflicts of interest through international law, and redistribute wealth to where it is most needed seems our best hope.

These arguments need improvement and refinement, but they are sufficiently substantive to provide us a guide in the twenty-first century.

Kant's Thesis on the Salutary Effects of Just Institutions: Immoral Man and Moral Society

The great American theologian and political realist Reinhold Niebuhr once wrote a book entitled *Moral Man and Immoral Society*,[35] arguing that while individuals were likely to be virtuous, the state was not. It lied, cheated, dissembled, and exploited other countries ruthlessly. Without denying Niebuhr's insights, I want to reinstate and defend a Kantian argument that the reverse is true. Individuals tend to be selfish, but society, at least in some parts of the world, has improved the quality of life of individuals and can be judged as morally superior to what it was in the past.

Stated formally, Kant defended two theses:

1. Individual human beings are and have always been selfish beings with limited sympathies who are biased toward their own interests.
2. Society has developed rules and customs to constrain and coordinate behavior, resulting in the improvement of the quality of our lives.

I begin with a simple example: Suppose you live in a community with few rules. Your neighbor's son Dexter buys a set of drums and begins to play them cacophonously at irregular periods of the day and night, resulting in loss of sleep, inability to concentrate, and a loathing for Dexter. Dexter's hobby has become your obsession. You approach Dexter's parents for help in this matter, but his mother tells you, "Dex has a right to play his drums whenever he likes."

Dexter's mother is right. There is no law prohibiting Dexter's drumming. So you appeal to your neighbors, calling a community meeting to express your grievance at 6 o'clock the next night. Almost everyone attends. In voicing your complaint, you discover that five other families are being disturbed by Dexter's drums and another five families are disturbed by loud piano playing at the other end of the block. Someone suggests a community rule that outlaws loud music except on designated occasions. A consensus accepts the rule and a system is put in place to enforce the rule. A system of hefty fines is put in place regarding anyone caught playing loud music or making loud noises for a sustained period of time. A judicial system is set up to deal with accused offenders and impose the fines. Dexter's parents, now having an incentive to constrain Dexter's freedom, find a far-off building where their son can play his drums without bothering anyone. Almost everyone is better off. Dexter's freedom has been constrained for the sake of the community.

Note that no one is more moral than before—certainly not Dexter, who resents the constraints—but the result is equivalent to Dexter becoming virtuous. Mutually agreed-upon, mutually coercive rules transform an anarchistic community into a civilized society.

This expansion of the law into civil life has the effect of gradually moralizing society. Morality requires that we follow right principles for their own sake (i.e., because reason enjoins them). Law mimics morality, externalizing the principles, supporting them with sanctions, and thus providing incentives to do what reason enjoins.

There are still sexists in Western societies, but the moral reasons for equal treatment of women has resulted in statutes condemning unjust discrimination against women. The enforcement of these laws—with heavy awards to victims of discrimination—has provided a disincentive to behave in a sexist manner. Sexist males continue to exist, but they have to disguise their behavior and tolerate the advancement of women in traditionally male professions. Equal rights are approximated in these societies.

A similar story can be told with regard to racism in the United States. In the 1960s, when Congress was debating Hubert Humphrey's proposed Civil Rights Act, it was widely argued that the act was ill advised. Opponents said, "You can't legislate morality." You can't change the racist heart by enacting laws.

They were probably right about morality, but they were wrong about the usefulness of the law. The Civil Rights Act of 1964 was passed by Congress, granting minority groups equal rights. It became illegal to discriminate in jobs, business, or university admission on the basis of race (or sex). Severe penalties were attached to racial discrimination, providing powerful disincentives to racist behavior. With the help of the media, the message got through: "Racism doesn't pay." Jim Crow laws in the segregated South gradually diminished. Blacks entered previously all-white universities, gained admission into the mainstream of the economy, and became integrated into all sectors of social life.[36] Honor codes serve in a similar manner to reduce cheating and dishonesty on college campuses. Institutions are a powerful tool for promoting moral behavior.

As American society expanded its horizons to include a previously excluded group, under the purview of civil rights, youth from hitherto racist families saw the wisdom of these laws, accepted them, and even argued with their parents about their racist ideas and behavior. The ideal of equal rights for all was gradually transformed from an external law to an internal moral norm. The opponents of the Civil Rights Act were wrong: To some extent it is possible to legislate morality and move from external sanctions to internal acceptance of a moral principle.

I am not arguing that law is an unmitigated blessing. There is a danger of overlegislation, of hairpin sensitivity to the offense in question— for example, suppose that an university, trying to promote respect for women, defines *sexual harassment* as "whatever makes a woman feel uncomfortable"; by this logic we could not give women low grades even if they deserved them—and of outlawing private acts that harm no one but may offend the tastes of the majority. The state can become a damned nuisance, intruding into people's private lives. It may be safest for the state to confine its laws to protecting our liberties (in general, enforcing negative rights, not positive duties to be virtuous).[37] In addition, excessive litigation can become a social curse. Long ago, Kant noted that "no straight thing had ever been constructed out of the crooked timber of humanity."[38] He was right. But abuse of a good institution doesn't invalidate the institution itself. Law remains the key to civilizing society. Laws have the potential to protect our liberties so that we can act autonomously and are free to live what we consider a good life.

This process of institutionalizing morality is the hope of humanity. We deliberate together in order to pass and enforce laws constraining immoral or annoying behavior. Then, once the laws are part of the culture, reason shows that they promote social utility and justice. Gradually, rational beings come to endorse the spirit of these laws, internalizing them, and conscience replaces the law in providing incentives to act morally. Instead of a police officer on every corner, which is prohibitively expensive and obtrusive, proper socialization instills an internal police officer into every conscious person. The anticipation of tormenting guilt prevents most immoral behavior.

Kant set forth the thesis that while human nature in our species has remained constant over time, humanity has made progress through its moral institutions.[39] People have always been self-centered social beings with limited sympathies. With some notable exceptions, they will act in accordance with their perceived self-interest, not the greater good of the community. Because we are social beings with limited abilities and resources, we need an ample amount of cooperation between persons in order to attain our goals. We must constrain our egoistic tendencies in order to ensure an adequate amount of cooperation for the common good.

Creating institutions in order to further our purposes is perhaps civilization's most advantageous invention. Morality, which serves to constrain our selfishness, is one of these fundamental institutions. We often take these rules for granted, and most of us who have been adequately socialized have the moral rules ingrained deeply within our psyches, so that they are an inextricable part of our personality. Similarly, institutions like etiquette and rituals provide common behavioral patterns to lubricate our social interactions. Law provides a more powerful instrument for behavior control because it assigns penalties to infractions.

Kant's point is that institutions such as laws and executive enforcement provide instruments to serve our moral purposes. Kant was far from being a utilitarian, but his message is a utilitarian one. The law provides the means for increasing aggregate welfare.

If we apply Kant's thesis to the Hobbesian predicament, we see why world government is a desideratum. Moral cosmopolitanism is unstable, needing institutional instantiation for the protection and advancement of human rights. Cosmopolitan reformers like Tom Pogge and Susan George have called on multinational corporations and nations to voluntarily tax themselves for the good of the worst-off people of the planet. But voluntary taxation is unlikely to find a warm welcome in those most able to contribute and tends, like charity in general, to impose burdens on the virtuous but lets the vicious and indifferent evade the requirements of justice. International law without enforcement fails to serve as law altogether.

Hence if the Kantian thesis on institutionalism is sound, moral cosmopolitans should be institutional cosmopolitans and commit themselves to end the Westphalian nation-state and bring into being a democratic world government dedicated to peace, justice, and well-being for all people everywhere. If this reasoning is correct, we must ask what kind of world government to institutionalize. Briefly, there are three types of world government:

1. Minimum World Government. States relinquish sovereignty over external relations but retain complete sovereignty over internal affairs.
2. Moderate World Government. States relinquish external sovereignty and some internal sovereignty (e.g., such as involving human rights) but retain substantial internal sovereignty.
3. Maximal World Government. States relinquish all external and internal sovereignty, so that the world government dominates all aspects of political life.

My proposal is to begin with minimal world government and gradually move to moderate world government. Maximal world government would be unwise and probably immoral. The US federal system or Swiss canton system, in which states have autonomy within the limits of the federal constitution, are examples of moderate world government that could be approximated on a global scale. We may designate this model soft nationalism within a broad cosmopolitan framework.

Soft Nationalism and Cosmopolitanism

There is truth in the claims of nationalism: Self-determination is a valid moral ideal and we do need to identify with groups such as the family and community and other associations in order to find meaning in life. It seems to be a natural, though limited, extension of the need for a sense of identification with our family to an identification with our nation. The nationalist rejects the cosmopolitan prescription of being a world citizen because the world is simply too large a body to identify with. But this may be a leap of scale. As Judith Lichtenberg points out, if I am not able to identify with 6 billion people, am I any more able to identify with the 270 million people in the United States?[40] Most humans can only identify with relatively small groups of fifty or a hundred, not anonymous millions. But while recognizing the problem that the nation is an artificial invention, it may nevertheless afford us a set of common symbols and cultural artifacts, such as a common language, literature, and history, which do promote human flourishing. So the meaning-identity analogy is plausible, after all. Seeing ourselves as part of a national team may be a valid way of seeing the useful function of the nation in giving our lives meaning and purpose. Lichtenberg's criticism, though literally valid, misses the point—nationalism has to do with symbols and meaning, not natural facts. All things considered, if a form of nationalism is morally justified, it will be a moderate, restricted form, one combined with cosmopolitanism.

Two related problems remain for the justification of nationalism, those of territory and of resources or property. Cosmopolitans criticize nationalists for their strong theory of property rights. Why should America or Saudi Arabia get a sole monopoly on their resources, which are just part of the natural lottery? Neither country did anything to deserve its superior natural resources; they were just more fortunate than less well-endowed countries. As such, would it not be fairer for the resources of these and all countries to be distributed more equitably? As Charles Beitz notes, "Resources do not stand in the same relation to personal identity as talents. It would be inappropriate to take the sort of pride in the diamond deposits in one's backyard that one takes in the ability to play *Appassionata*."[41] Of course, being good stewards of our resources, including sharing them with the needy, may justify some ownership.

In a world government, nations might be designated stewards of their land and resources, but not permitted complete sovereignty over their uses. Richer nations would have a duty to redistribute some of their wealth to those poorer nations in which people's basic needs were not met. The United States, with a gross domestic product of over $2.6 trillion, gives only about 0.01 percent of this to developing countries in terms of nonmilitary aid. If morality is inherently cosmopolitan, we should be working harder to aid poorer people in less developed countries. Peter Singer argues from a utilitarian perspective that "[i]f it is in our power to prevent something bad from happening, without thereby sacrificing something of comparable moral importance, we ought to do it."[42] What changes would we need to make in our lifestyles if we attempted to live according to Singer's challenge? However, until such a cosmopolitan regime is established, it is hard to see either nations or individuals giving up sovereignty to their territory and resources. Even though Beitz's point about resources versus talents is cogent, nations do behave as though their resources were analogous to talents, and convincing them otherwise will be a difficult job. It may not succeed, but it is worth trying. I for one believe it will eventually occur.

Cosmopolitanism appears to be a worthy ideal, embodying, as it does, the moral point of view in respecting individuals as the centers of meaning rather than nations, races, religious, or ethnic groups, but the ideal is fraught with seemingly insuperable problems. First, what kind of institution would be required to draw up and enforce the global scheme of taxation required for the kinds of wealth redistribution schemes that might be warranted? Would the coercive power of such an institution be an unacceptable violation of individual and national liberties? Second, even if we could ensure a just world government to carry out a taxation scheme, how could we be certain that the funds distributed actually went to the poor and were not siphoned off by a corrupt elite and deposited into their Swiss bank accounts, as happens all too frequently with foreign aid to developing countries? Third, how do we guarantee that after funds get to the poor, long-term good would result from the redistribution scheme?

These difficulties lead the leading political philosopher of our generation, John Rawls, to reject the possibility of world government that "would either be a global despotism or else would rule over a fragile empire torn by frequent civil strife as various regions and peoples tried to gain their political freedom and autonomy."[43]

Rawls provides no argument or evidence for this sweeping judgment. Certainly, the development of cosmopolitan institutions with sufficient checks and balances to prevent any tendency toward despotism will take time and effort, but as Plato said long ago, nothing great has ever been built without great difficulty.

Similarly, Rawls' fears about world government being fraught with the threat of anarchy seems a contingent matter. Just as the federation of fifty states into a single nation, the United States of America, has survived without falling into chaos (though it was threatened by the terrible Civil War), so is there reason to believe a harmonious relationship of the world states could eventually become a reality.

A fourth problem concerns how one can compare what constitutes a good life in different kinds of societies. The per-capita gross domestic product of many Western counties is around $25,000, whereas in the third world it may be around $250, one hundred times less. Someone from a third world country, say, an Amazonian Indian in Brazil, may not value college education as much as Westerners do and may live in a tribe that has a pattern of caring for the elderly, obviating the need for expensive retirement policies. In fact, the Amazonian Indian, upon being exposed to Western culture, may prefer to remain living in the rain forest.

These problems may not be insuperable, but they should give us pause. Until we understand the full implications of what we are doing, a move toward institutionalizing cosmopolitanism should proceed cautiously. Nonetheless, the principle of humanity, embodied in the moral point of view, which focuses on the rights and duties of individuals rather than groups, races, or nations, does point to a robust cosmopolitanism that could be institutionalized into a democratic world government.

A fifth problem related to international relations concerns intervention in the internal affairs of nation-states, such as that occurring in Somalia, Afghanistan, Rwanda, Malawi, Serbia, Kosovo, and Iraq when human rights violations such as the oppression of women and "ethnic cleansing" became extreme. Even if we accept the principle of national sovereignty, intervention by other nations is sometimes justified. The widespread ethnic cleansing that took place in the former Yugoslavia in the 1990s is a prime example of when the intervention of other nations might be warranted. Working out the criteria for when to intervene and when not to is one of the most urgent problems facing us. We want to be constructive, rather than adding to the destruction in these war-torn lands, but it is notoriously difficult to determine the likelihood of success. Such interventions are risky and should be embarked upon only when all attempts at peaceful solutions have been exhausted, when there is widespread international support, when there is willingness for a long-term occupancy, and when there is a reasonable chance of success.

Cosmopolitan institutions threaten the very existence of the traditional nation-state, so much a part of our world since the eighteenth century. If our ultimate allegiance is to a superglobal state, then what is the role of the nation? Does it have moral legitimacy?

Many philosophers would say no; the nation lacks any ultimate moral justification. It is, at best, a temporary and necessary evil, organizing people in restricted manners until the principle of universal humanity can take hold on our collective consciousness. Einstein once quipped that nationalism is an infantile disease, "the measles of mankind" from which we must recover if we are to survive. But, as our analysis suggests, this may be an unnecessarily harsh reaction. Certainly, there is a hard version of nationalism—epitomized in the slogan "My country, right or wrong!"—that is not justified because it makes nationalism into an absolute, something that cannot be justified. Such extreme nationalism is no more justified than giving special privilege to one's race or gender or ethnic group. We have an obligation to oppose our country when it violates human rights, even as some Germans, like the martyrs and resisters Dietrich Bonhoeffer and Adam von Trapp, opposed Hitler's Nazism. We must transcend this kind of extreme, immoral nationalism, with its atavistic rituals and narrow patriotism, and replace it with a universal loyalty. There is a prima facie duty to become moral cosmopolitans, committed to the well-being and rights of every person, regardless of country of origin. There are practical obstacles to overcome, as well as moral ones, so we cannot immediately move into such an international allegiance, but this should be our goal. Moral cosmopolitanism, treating each person as a moral equal, is not equivalent to institutional cosmopolitanism, but it inclines in that direction. The benefits of world government are greater prospects of peace, enforcement of treaties and contracts, fluid trade and economic relations, and the allocation of resources according to need and desert, rather than according to purely the luck of being born in a resource-rich country or family.

But cosmopolitanism is not without problems. It has a checkered past and many associate it with frightening prospects of George Orwell's tyrannical *1984* and world dictatorship depicted in Aldous Huxley's *Brave New World*. Marxist-Leninism purported to be the ultimate cosmopolitan philosophy, and it gave rise to the USSR, the completely "internationalist" society, and the atrocities of Stalin. It is estimated that Stalin was responsible for the deaths of more than 50 million people. Cosmopolitanism can be a veneer for tyranny. Cosmopolitanism seems more appealing on a micro scale of political organization than a macro scale.[44] We should commit ourselves to equal universal human rights, but not necessarily to universal world government. But even on the micro level, dangers and distortions abound. The nineteenth-century cosmopolitan William Godwin held that if two persons are drowning and one is a relative of yours, then it should make no difference in your decision as to whom to try to rescue first.[45] But our particularist commitments to family and friends would prescribe otherwise. Charles Dickens satirizes this "telescopic philanthropy" in the person of Mrs. Jelleby, who, neglecting her family, could only recognize objects of benevolence at a very great distance: "Mrs Jelleby's eyes had the curious habit of looking a long way off. As if they could see nothing nearer than Africa."[46] It was said of President Woodrow Wilson that he loved mankind but loathed individual men. Commonsense morality, as we noted above, informs us that demanding misplaced altruism undermines the very substance of morality found in those personal relationships that make life worth living. It is our basic communitarian values that constitute the bases of moral sentiments. To this extent, the particularists are correct. Our love and moral commitments must begin and always remain tied to particular people, not humanity in the abstract. Furthermore, as soft nationalists point out, we may take legitimate pride in our democratic institutions, our practices of equality before the law and moral traditions. These aspects of our culture are worth preserving and defending. From a moral point of view, all cultures are not equal. Some instantiate the ideals better than others.

At this point, we might compromise and recognize the validity of both cosmopolitanism and nationalism. Nationalists may be divided into two groups: *soft nationalists* and *hard nationalists*. Hard nationalists hold that the nation is altogether justified as the ultimate locus of political obligation, so internationalism is simply confused or immoral. Even as we have a natural duty to prefer our family to other people and strangers, we have a duty to prefer our nation, to be patriotic. Nationalistic concerns override all other loyalties or obligations. On the other hand, soft nationalists maintain that while we do have some obligations to people everywhere and we need some adjudicating overseer to enforce treaties and prevent war, this doesn't completely override the need for nation-states. They agree with hard nationalists that we do have special obligations to our own country, but soft nationalists feel that the needs or rights of others may sometimes override our familial obligations, and that our nationalistic obligations may be overridden at times by obligations to humankind at large or to people not citizens of our nation. Cosmopolitanism is a form of soft nationalism.

Conclusion

Globalism makes world government possible and a recognition of universal human rights makes it desirable: The synthesis makes it actual. We might set down the argument of this paper as follows:

1. The moral point of view entails universal human rights.
2. Human rights require institutionalization for their full realization.
3. Because of the Hobbesian state of nature among nations, institutional cosmopolitanism (world government) offers the best opportunity for supporting human rights.
4. Therefore, the moral point of view leads to support of institutional cosmopolitanism (world government).
5. Globalism offers the resources to realize the moral point of view in an institutional manner.

Today the ideas of a global economy, a planetary environment, a world health organization, and a World Wide Web are accepted without much demur. But still to be accepted is a concept closely related to these concepts, that of a single human society. Unless this universal idea is recognized and acted upon, these other concepts will not be able to be applied and the human species will continue to be threatened by disease, famine, war, and terrorism. Some time ago, the Catholic priest and paleontologist Teilhard de Chardin wrote, "Love one another or perish. . . . We have reached the critical path in human evolution in which the only path open to us is to move toward a common passion, a *conspiracy of love*."[47] Moral institutions have the promise of institutionalizing the conspiracy of love so that it translates into a world of greater peace and justice.

Because it offers us a special form of personal relationship so vital for personal identity, some form of nationalism may always be part of the human psyche, though it may be a less all-encompassing variety than what we now experience. It will be balanced by a soft form of cosmopolitanism, either informally worked out between nations or by a formal world government that will still encourage and promote individual nation-state autonomy within its domain. World government seems a viable solution to the problems that the nine forces moving us toward globalism are creating: environmental pollution, health hazards, increased ease of transportation, communication and migration, the need for international law and the regulation of unclaimed geography and outer space, cultural and linguistic confrontations, the growth of multinational corporations in a world market, and, especially, concerns about peace and security. John Maynard Keynes, in the passage quoted in the epigraph at beginning of this chapter, reminded us that the wildest ideas of philosophers, rejected as absurd in their time, have sometimes become the orthodoxy of the future. My thesis has been that forces exist and morality supports the realization of the cosmopolitan ideal in the future development of international relations.[48]

Notes

1. David Carment, "The Ethnic Dimension in World Politics," *Third World Quarterly* 15, no. 4 (1994): 551–82.
2. The Declaration of Independence, 1776.
3. Michael Walzer, *Spheres of Justice* (New York: Basic, 1983), p. 39.
4. David Miller, *On Nationality* (Oxford: Oxford University Press, 1995); Michael Sandel, *Liberalism and the Limits of Justice* (New York: Cambridge University Press, 1982); Nel Noddings, *Care: A Feminist Approach to Ethics and Moral Education* (Berkeley and Los Angeles: University of California Press, 1986); Alasdair MacIntyre, "Is Patriotism a Virtue?" in *Political Philosophy: Classic and Contemporary Readings*, edited by L. Pojman (New York: McGraw-Hill, 2002).
5. Amos Oz, *In the Land of Israel* (New York: Vintage, 1983), pp. 130f.
6. Alfred Lord Tennyson, "Locksley Hall," l. 125–28. (First printed in 1842.)
7. Isaiah 11:6–9, 2:4.
8. Galatians 3:28.
9. See George Sabine, *A History of Political Theory* (Hillside, IL: Dryden, 1973), pp. 243–48.
10. L. Pojman, *Political Philosophy: Classic and Contemporary Readings*. For a good discussion of this essay, see Stephen Nathanson, *Patriotism, Morality, and Peace* (Lanham, MD: Rowman & Littlefield, 1993), chaps. 1 and 2.
11. See Jacques Maritain, *Man and the State* (Washington, DC: Catholic University Press, 1950).
12. William Greider, *One World, Ready or Not: The Manic Logic of Global Capitalism* (New York: Simon & Schuster, 1997), p. 11.

13. The list looks like this:

Rank Company and Nation-State Revenues
($ millions)

1.	United States	1,946,000.0
2.	Germany	802,000.0
3.	United Kingdom	565,000.0
4.	Italy	504,000.0
5.	Japan	441,000.0
6.	France	286,000.0
7.	Wal-Mart Stores	246,525.0
8.	China	224,500.0
9.	GeneralMotors	186,763.0
10.	Exxon Mobil	182,466.0
11.	Royal Dutch/Shell Group	179,431.0
12.	BP	178,721.0
13.	Canada	178,600.0
14.	Ford Motor	163,871.0
15.	DaimlerChrysler	141,421.1
16.	Mexico	136,000.0
17.	Netherlands	134,000.0
18.	Toyota Motor	131,754.2
19.	General Electric	131,698.0
20.	Sweden	119,000.0
21.	South Korea	118,100.0
22.	Belgium	113,400.0
23.	Mitsubishi	109,386.1
24.	Mitsui	108,630.7
25.	Spain	105,000.0
26.	Allianz Insurance	101,930.2
27.	Citigroup	100,789.0
28.	Brazil	100,600.0

From *Fortune*, July 21, 2003, http://www.fortune.com/fortune/lists/F500/index.html. Surprisingly, Russia, with a GDP of $70 billion, is not in the top thirty richest companies/nations.

14. "Its [Exxon's] 195 ocean-going tankers, owned and chartered, constitute a private navy as big as Britain's." Anthony J. Parisi, "How Exxon Rules Its Great Empire," *San Francisco Chronicle*, August 5, 1980, quoted in William H. Shaw and Vincent Barry, eds., *Moral Issues in Business*, 5th ed. (Belmont, CA: Wadsworth, 1992), p. 202.

15. David Korten, *When Corporations Rule the World* (San Francisco: Bartlett-Koehler, 2001), p. 126.

16. Paraphrased from George Monbiot, *Manifesto for a New World Order* (New York: New Press, 2004), p. 226.

17. Korten, *When Corporations Rule the World*, p. 107.

18. Susan George, "Globalizing Rights," in *Globalizing Rights: The Oxford Amnesty Lectures 1999*, edited by Matthew Gibney (New York: Oxford University Press, 2003).

19. Thomas Friedman, *The Lexus and the Olive Tree* (New York: Farrar, Straus, and Giroux, 1999), p. 7.

20. Friedman, *The Lexus and the Olive Tree*, pp. 26–27. But what happens when those fighting over the olive tree suddenly discover that the true enemy of their traditional ways of life is not their historic opponent, but a vast, impersonal, multinational complex? This is what the antitechnology movement is all about. See also Michael Hardt and Antonio Negri, *Empire* (Cambridge, MA: Harvard University Press, 2000).

21. Matthew Gibney, ed., *Globalizing Rights: The Oxford Amnesty Lectures 1999* (New York: Oxford University Press, 2003), p. 1.

22. Thomas Hobbes, *Leviathan*, part 2, chapter 17.

23. Raymond Williams, *Towards 2000* (London: Chatto & Windus, 1982).

24. I owe this point to the biologist John Jagger.

25. See Dennis Altman, *Global Sex* (Chicago: University of Chicago Press, 2001) for a comprehensive treatment of the spread of Western sexual mores.

26. See Benjamin Barber, "Jihad vs. McWorld," *Atlantic Monthly*, March 1992.

27. See Garrett Harding's classic article, "The Tragedy of the Commons," *Science* 162 (December 1986).

28. FBI director Louis Freeh's statement before the U.S. Congress, April 21, 1992.

29. Thomas Hobbes, *Leviathan*, chap. 13.

30. Cicero, *De Officiis*, bk. 1, sec. 11, chap. 34 [44bc].

31. Thomas Hobbes, "A Letter Concerning Toleration," 1706.

32. The passage from Isaiah 11 quoted earlier would seem to indicate that cosmopolitanism should include significant animal rights, but for purposes of this paper I will confine my discussion to human rights.

33. For a fuller defense of these theses, see my *Ethics: Discovering Right and Wrong* (Belmont, CA: Wadsworth, 2004).

34. See www.gatesfoundation.org/GlobalHealth.

35. Reinhold Niebuhr, *Moral Man and Immoral Society* (New York: Macmillan, 1980).

36. This is not to deny that racism still is a problem. Witness Randy Weaver, target of the Ruby Ridge raid by US marshalls, who said, "The word 'racist' is

a good word; it means be proud of your race." *Ruby Ridge*, Discovery/Times Channel, broadcast May 22, 2004. The question is, How is racism different from nationalism?

37. In *On Liberty* (1861) John Stuart Mill set forth the Harm Principle, which contains general criterion for laws: "That principle is, that the sole end for which mankind are warranted, individually or collectively in interfering with the liberty of action of any of their number, is self-protection. The only purpose for which power can be rightfully exercised over any member of a civilized community, against his will, is to prevent harm to others."

38. Isaiah Berlin, *The Crooked Timber of Humanity: Chapters in the History of Ideas* (New York: Alfred Knopf, 1991), p. xi.

39. "Idea for a Universal History with Cosmopolitan Purpose," in *Kant: Political Writings*, edited by Hans Reiss (New York: Cambridge University Press, 1970).

40. Judith Lichtenberg, "Nationalism; For and (Mainly) Against," in Robert McKim and Jeff McMahan, *The Morality of Nationalism* (New York: Oxford University Press, 1997), p. 161.

41. Charles Beitz, *Political Theory and International Relations* (Princeton, NJ: Princeton University Press, 1999), p. 139.

42. Peter Singer, "Famine, Affluence and Morality," *Philosophy and Public Affairs* 1, no. 3 (1972).

43. John Rawls, *The Law of the Peoples* (Cambridge, MA: Harvard University Press, 1999), p. 36.

44. One problem endemic to all large bureaucracies is that of runaway perks. Recent studies show that the members of the European Parliament can and often do quadruple their salaries through special allowances for travel and language learning. ("In Europe's Parliament, a Fondness for the Perks," *New York Times*, May 24, 2004.)

45. Robert McKim and Jeff McMahan, *The Morality of Nationalism* (New York: Oxford University Press, 1997), p. 161.

46. Charles Dickens, *Bleak House* (London: Bradbury and Evans, 1853), p. 26.

47. Quoted in Ivan Head and Pierre Elliott Trudeau, *The Canadian Way: Shaping Canada's Foreign Policy 1968–1984* (Toronto: McCelland & Stewart, 1995).

48. I am indebted to Robert Audi, Michael Brough, Chris Fitter, Stephen Kershnar, John Jagger, Jonathan Harrison, Sterling Harwood, James Kellenberger, Bruce Landesman, Ruth Pojman, Robert Chenciner, Joseph Runzo, Mylan Engel, John Kleinig, and Morton Winston for comments on previous versions of this chapter.

3

On Human Rights

On the Universal Declaration of Human Rights

O N December 10, 1948, the General Assembly of the United Nations adopted and proclaimed the Universal Declaration of Human Rights as a set of ideals that should guide social and economic behavior in the complex, shrinking postwar global village. These rights and freedoms are universal, applying to all human beings everywhere regardless of race, color, sex, or national or social origin (Art. 2). They include the usual "rights to life and liberty" but add such economic rights as "the right to work" and "the right of equal pay for equal work" (Art. 23), and such welfare rights as "social security" (Art. 23) and a decent standard of living (Art. 25). It will be instructive to understand how this document came about.

The main catalyst for such a document was widespread revulsion at the Nazi atrocities, especially the holocaust, and the Japanese torture of prisoners during World War II. After the controversial Nuremberg Trials, which technically were dealing with ex post facto law, clear international guidelines were thought to be needed to help prevent anyone *in the future* from claiming ignorance as an excuse for committing atrocities. Similarly, Article 14, on the right to asylum from political persecution, had in mind the fact that thousands of Jews attempting to flee Germany in the late 1930s and during the war were turned away from other countries. Article 21, stating that "everyone has the right to take part in the government of his country or through freely chosen representatives," was in response to the antidemocratic, fascist regimes of Germany, Italy, and Japan. Articles 19 and 20, on free speech, were tailored in such a way as to tolerate speech that would not have been tolerated in fascist countries. The first two articles hold to the moral equality of all humans and urge a spirit of brotherhood. Article 2 sums up the antidiscrimination thesis that runs throughout the declaration:

> Everyone is entitled to all the rights and freedoms set forth in this Declaration, without distinction of any kind, such as race, color, sex, language, religion, political or other opinion, national or social origin, property, birth or other status. Furthermore, no distinction shall be made on the basis of the political, jurisdictional or international status of the country or territory to which a person belongs, whether it be independent, trust, non-self-governing or under any other limitation of sovereignty.

The discussion of the various points often refer to Hitler's *Mein Kampf,* which is taken as the epitome of what the declaration is intended to combat. For example, in his book Hitler had dismissed individual conscience as a "Jewish invention." The writers of the declaration had this contempt for conscience in mind when they proclaimed in the preamble that "disregard and contempt for human rights had resulted in barbarous acts which had outraged the conscience of mankind." Under the direction of Adolf Eichmann, German lawyers had drawn up legislation stripping Jews of citizenship. Johannes Morsink comments, "To be without a nationality or not be a citizen of any country at all is to stand naked in the world of international affairs. It is to be alone as a person, without protection against the aggression of states, an unequal battle which the individual is bound to lose."[1] As a result of this revulsion against Nazi law, Article 15 was adopted: "Everyone has a right to nationality." The common denominator uniting the delegates was their outrage at Hitler's ideas and actions and their determination to sound a clear message opposing them. Their sentiments took on a universal form. Generalizing, we can say that the purpose of the Declaration of Human Rights was to protect all human beings from oppression, torture, exploitation, and enslavement.

The second catalyst for the declaration was President Franklin Roosevelt's four universal freedoms (freedom of speech and religion, and from want and fear), stated in his 1941 State of the Union message to

Congress. They were viewed as the forerunner of such a declaration, a sort of mini-declaration. Fittingly, President Harry Truman asked Roosevelt's widow, Eleanor Roosevelt, to head the United States' delegation to the Commission on Human Rights. She became the leitmotif, the driving force and chairwoman of the committee charged with drawing up a universal document on human rights. The document was based on an initial draft by John P. Humphrey, a Canadian law professor and newly appointed director of the UN Secretariat's Division on Human Rights. René Cassin, a French scholar, organized and revised the first draft. Mrs. Roosevelt ably guided the process through two years of vigorous disputation and further revision. The USSR objected to some of the principles and insisted on Article 22, the right to social security.[2] The document is an example of *soft law* as opposed to *hard law*. Whereas hard law (sometimes called black-letter law) is the law of the courts, soft law is informal law, setting forth ideals that constrain our behavior and may in time become hard law. The Universal Declaration of Human Rights, as a document of soft law, has become the most important document on international human rights ever written, already influential in legal cases and exerting a moral force, constraining international behavior. It was eventually passed by the members of the UN Commission on Human Rights by a vote of 38 to 0, with eight nations abstaining, including the USSR and four of its satellite countries, Saudi Arabia, and apartheid-divided South Africa. The Soviet bloc would have voted against the declaration, but realized that a negative vote would have drawn attention to Stalin's purges, which might be compared with the Nazi Holocaust. So, thanks to the able and dedicated leadership of Eleanor Roosevelt, the declaration passed. It has become the guiding document of human rights organizations like Amnesty International and Human Rights Watch, and was used to exert moral pressure on the proapartheid leaders of South Africa.

Initially much skepticism attended the creation of this document. One of the first opponents was the American Anthropological Association (AAA), which in 1947 sent a memorandum to the UN Commission on Human Rights warning of the likelihood of ethnocentrism, which is "[s]o subtle, and its effects so far-reaching, that only after considerable training are we conscious of it."[3]

---

1. The individual realizes his personality through his culture, hence respect for individual differences entails respect for cultural differences.

2. Respect for differences between cultures is validated by the scientific fact that no technique of qualitatively evaluating cultures has been discovered.

3. Standards and values are relative to the culture from which they derive so that any attempt to formulate postulates that grow out of the belief or moral codes of one culture must to that extent detract from the applicability of any Declaration of Human Rights to mankind as a whole.[4]

This argument from cultural diversity for ethical relativism supposes that all values are justified by their dependency on cultural acceptance. The implication is that, since cultures are radically different from one another, the construction of any Universal Declaration of Human Rights is a contradiction in terms and should not be attempted.

Let us examine this argument. Premise 1 seems true. We are conditioned by our culture. Premise 2 is partly true, but partly problematic. It is true that science hasn't found a way to prove that one culture is superior to another. But this ignores the fact that moral philosophy has developed rational principles that need to be examined on their own merit. The first clause of this premise is problematic because, after denying universal values, it urges universal respect for all cultures. The problem is that I may live in a culture that is intolerant toward other cultures, so that if cultural acceptance is the only justification of a moral principle, it would be immoral for us to respect other cultures. Premise 3 is doubtful, neglecting the fact/value distinction. Simply because I learn my morality from my culture does not entail that it is the true morality. I may be ignorant of objective values that other cultures embody. Just as in medicine, culture A may be ignorant of a therapy aiding the cure of a deadly disease like AIDS, which is widely used in another culture, B, so culture A may be ignorant of a valid moral principle that is widely adhered to in another culture B. One of the values of multicultural dialogue is to reason together in order to develop or discover a set of principles that we can all accept. These principles will have to be seen to be in the basic interest of people of every culture, even as they impose obligations on people of every culture. Deontologists, utilitarians, evolutionary ethicists, and contractualists, in different ways, have come up with a wide range of principles of this sort containing a *common core* of principles serving as an overlapping consensus.[5] Such principles include negative duties to refrain from arbitrarily harming others, the principle of reciprocity (if someone helps you, repay him or her in kind), and promise keeping, all of which are vital for any successful social cohesion.

If this is true, if a minimal set of moral principles can be discovered that are acceptable to rational human beings of every culture, then this set of principles can form the basis for universal human rights. One problem of rights advocates has been to make it appear that rights just "appear," as self-standing, self-evident truths, which they are not. Rights are derived from a wider moral theory that centers on a theory of obligation. It is not because you have an independent right to food or security that I should feed or protect you; it is because we have general duties to help those in need that you have a prima facie right to be fed and protected. Thus we may reject the AAA's ethnocentric argument as unsound.

A second objection came from the Soviet delegate to the Commission on Human Rights, Andrei Vyshinsky, who was the prosecutor of the infamous Stalin purge trials that resulted in the torture and executions of thousands of political enemies. He argued that "[h]uman rights could not be conceived outside the state; the very concept of right and law was connected with that of the State."[6] Other USSR delegates continually set forth amendments to the various principles making the state the repository of rights.[7] Of course, this version of relativism, substituting the political institution for the cultural one, accepted in the USSR as a tenet of Marxist ideology, would have undermined the whole raison d'être of the declaration, that is, to serve as a deterrent to and prevent the recurrence of such actions as the Holocaust. It was precisely the need to make a statement against state tyranny and abuse of human beings that prompted the United Nations to embark on the task of drawing up universal principles. The universalist position is that our common humanity, though contextualized within cultures and states, is more fundamental than either and can be the basis of a rationally justified set of basic duties and rights. Slavery is wrong even if a culture or state approves of it. Putting Jews, Gypsies, and other innocent people into gas ovens is morally wrong even though the state approves it and the culture accepts it. Depriving people of freedom without an overriding moral justification is also wrong, even if a culture is unaware of the ideal.

The declaration sets forth the essential negative and positive rights of people who wish to live a minimally decent life. It grants the classic negative rights of freedom of speech and opinion and from slavery, servitude, and arbitrary coercion. But it also grants some minimal positive rights, such as food, clothing, shelter, and basic medical care, which seem necessary for the enjoyment of the other rights, for it is difficult to see how anyone can enjoy the right to free speech or political participation if he or she has not eaten for several days, is homeless, is searching in the garbage for a winter coat, or has not received medical treatment for a debilitating disease, all for reasons beyond his or her control. Certain subsistence rights such as the right to food, clean water, and shelter are necessary minimal requirements for a good life.

Not all of the articles of the declaration are of equal merit. Article 1, "Everyone has the right to life, liberty and security of person," and Article 2, promoting nondiscrimination, seem clear and basic; those like Article 24, giving everyone the right to leisure and "periodic holidays with pay"; Article 25, declaring that everyone has a right to medical care; and Article 22, advocating the right to social security, may be possible to implement only in societies with well-developed economic, political, and educational standards and policies.

Maurice Cranston has argued that the declaration has a utopian ring to it that may deflect from its genuine validity. He points out that the first half of the declaration correctly identifies the rights already widely recognized by the majority of people in the world, even if they do not observe them, but the second half sets forth "supposed" ones that are not yet real, but only ideals that will depend on the economic and social development of humanity.[8] This is a valid point, but the proponents may accept it and respond that we ought to be working for a world in which these rights can be actualized.

Nonetheless, it seems remarkable that a group of forty-six people from very different cultures, from Soviet Communist, Islamic, Japanese, and Chinese, to European, Latin American, North American, and the Pacific Island countries, would come to the consensus they did. The declaration may well be the most important moral work of the twentieth century, for it is the first international declaration of human rights and embodies the core of objective morality necessary for any civilized community. It has served as the basis for moral guidance and international sanctions for more than fifty years and hopefully will continue to find realization in the lives of people everywhere.

What Are Rights?

It is because of their protective importance that we need to ask: What precisely are rights? Where do rights come from? Are there any natural rights, rights that do not depend on social contract, prior moral duties, utilitarian outcomes, or ideals?

Although there is a great deal of variation in defining *rights* in the literature, for our purposes we can say that a right is a claim against others that at the same time includes a liberty on one's own behalf.[9] J. L. Mackie captures this combination when he writes, "A right, in the most important sense, is a conjunction of a freedom and a claim-right. That is, if someone, A, has the moral right to do X, not only is he entitled to do X if he chooses—he is not morally required not to do X—but he is also protected in his doing of X—others are morally required not to interfere or prevent him."[10]

There are dangers in moving toward a strong commitment to human rights. Because rights give us good things, they are more attractive than their correlative duties. Because the notion of rights allows us to make claims, the language can be co-opted by greedy and self-serving people trying to weasel out of their responsibilities. For example, Warren and Patricia Simpson, a couple in Montclair, New Jersey, declared that they're not very good at child rearing and don't much like it, so they're exercising their *right* to retire from it. "Between the crying and the fighting and asking for toys, it was getting to be very discouraging," Mrs. Simpson said. "We're both still young, and we have a lot of other interests." They've put their three small children up for adoption and, after seven years of parenting, they "are moving on."[11] Almost every day we hear of a new set of rights being proposed or instituted to serve some group's interest: patients' rights, homeowners' rights, animal rights, the rights of trees. Lately, student athletes dissatisfied with the restrictions of the NCAA on their ability to market their talents have proposed a Student-Athletes' Bill of Rights, which would permit them to secure "employment not associated with his/her amateur sport," such as doing advertisements for hire.[12] No doubt many rights claims are warranted, but their very proliferation as claims for being fundamental moral entities may be causing an inflation, devaluing the currency of rights.[13] Groups extend rights to animals, to corporations, and to forests. Such extensions to new groups may or may not be justified, but the case for the extension must be carefully argued. Not everyone who claims a right to X has a legitimate case for X. Nevertheless, almost all rights systems grant human beings the rights of life, liberty, property, and the pursuit of happiness. The fact that rights language can be abused is not a sufficient reason to renounce its valid use.

How to Justify Human Rights

Several attempts have been made to provide a theoretical justification of human rights. These can be divided into top-down and bottom-up theories. Top-down justifications begin with a general moral principle or overriding reason whence rights are derived. John Locke held that God created us and all the earth for our enjoyment, endowing us with rights to life, liberty, and property.[14] Immanuel Kant's categorical imperative is a classic philosophical principle from which duties and rights may be derived, so long as they pass the universalizability test. In the Kantian tradition lies Alan Gewirth's metajustification of human rights. In his book *Reason and Morality*, his essay "Epistemology of Human Rights," and elsewhere, Gewirth argues that we can infer equal human rights to freedom and well-being from the notion of rational agency.[15] A broad outline of the argument is as follows: Each rational agent must recognize that a measure of freedom and well-being is necessary for his or her exercise of rational agency. That is, each rational agent must will, if he is to will at all, that he possess that measure of freedom and well-being. Therefore, anyone who holds that freedom and well-being are necessary for his or her exercise of rational agency is logically committed to holding that he or she has a prudential right to these goods. By the principle of universalizability we obtain the conclusion that all rational agents have a prima facie *right* to freedom and well-being. In this way Gewirth seeks to establish minimal human rights.

But Gewirth's argument is invalid. From the premise that I need freedom and well-being in order to exercise my will, nothing follows by itself concerning a right to freedom and well-being. From the fact that I assert a need or prudential right to some X does not give anyone else a sufficient reason to grant me that X. Needs don't generate moral rights.

But even if we can make sense of Gewirth's argument, this would at best give us not a notion of equal rights based on equal human worth, but merely minimal equal prima facie rights to freedom and well-being, which could be overridden for other reasons. Inegalitarians like Aristotle could accept this kind of equal right and argue that the prima facie right to minimal freedom of action should be overridden either when the actions are irrational or when a hierarchically structured society has need of slaves, in which case those who were best suited to this role would have their prima facie right to free action suitably constrained. In like manner utilitarians could accept Gewirthian equal prima facie rights and override them whenever greater utility was at stake. Gewirthian equal rights reduce to little more than recognizing that noninterference and well-being are values we have a prima facie moral duty to promote, whether in animals or angels, humans or Galacticans. But they don't give us a set of thick natural rights.

Reacting to such failures as Gewirth's, philosophers like Richard Rorty have embraced a relativist solution to the problem of human rights, thus robbing them of any universality. Rorty argues that what the cause of human rights needs is passion and courage, not reason and theory.[16] But passion and courage can work both ways, as the terrorist suicide bombers have shown us. Another leading human rights activist, Jack Donnelly, has opted for a consensus strategy. He writes that human rights are "almost universally accepted," at least as ideal standards. But of course there is no universal consensus, as the recent events in Rwanda, Serbo-Croatia, and the Middle East have demonstrated. So we are back with ethical relativism.[17]

In light of the failure of relativism and top-down strategies, a bottom-up strategy may be more promising. Specifically, a more hopeful way to look at the Universal Declaration of Human Rights may be to regard it as a set of rules generated upward from experience within a broad rule-utilitarian framework. They are practical injunctions that, if followed, would lead to great overall happiness or human flourishing. They are not dropped out of heaven or self-evident rational principles, but human inventions, what John Searle calls "social constructions," ideas that have great social utility, especially if everyone abides by them. We assign a status function Y to a certain object X for utilitarian purposes. For example, we issue a little plastic card (X) labeled "driver's license" to motorists who have passed a driving test, enabling them legally to drive in that country (Y). Similarly, we issue paper deeds (X) to people giving them rights to own property (Y). A famous example of a social construction is money. Searle describes the invention this way:

> The story told about Medieval Europe is that bankers would accept gold and store it for safekeeping, and in return for the gold they issued paper certificates to the depositors of the gold. The certificates then could be used as a medium of exchange, just as the gold itself was. The certificate was a kind of substitute for the gold. It had complete credibility as an object of value, because at any point it was exchangeable for gold. . . . A stroke of genius occurred when somebody figured out that we can increase the supply of money simply by issuing more certificates than we have gold. As long as the certificates continue to function, as long as they have a collectively imposed function that continues to be collectively accepted, the certificates are, as they say, as good as gold. The next stroke of genius came when somebody figured out—and it took a long time for people to figure this out—we can forget about the gold and just have certificates. With this change we have arrived at fiat money, and this is the situation we are in today.[18]

The steps from a mere piece of paper to a piece of paper signifying a substitute for gold to "this paper signifies a certain amount of purchasing power in the economy" require the collective endorsement of the community. We create social reality, but it is a purposeful creation, one that serves our purposes. Searle applies this bottom-up approach to the creation of morality and human rights. Just as money (X) serves our economic purposes as a fungible tool for exchange of goods (Y), so moral principles (X), including human rights, are functional rules for coordinating behavior (Y). Searle puts it this way:

> Prior to the European Enlightenment the concept of rights had application only within some institutional structure—property rights, marital rights, droit de seigneur, etc. But somehow the idea came to be collectively accepted that one might have a status-function solely by virtue of being a human being, that the X term was "human" and the Y term was "possessor of inalienable rights." It is no accident that the collective acceptance of this move was aided by the idea of divine authority: "they are endowed by their Creator with certain unalienable rights, that among these are Life, Liberty, and the pursuit of Happiness." The idea of human rights has survived the decline of religious belief, and has even become internationalized. The Helsinki Declaration on Human Rights is frequently appealed to, with varying degrees of effectiveness, against dictatorial regimes. Lately

there has even been a movement for the recognition of animal rights. Both human and animal rights are cases of the imposition of status-function through collective intentionality.[19]

In sum, human rights are social constructs that develop out of our moral understanding of how to build a better world. We invent them because, like paper money or the wheel, they are socially useful. Once invented, they take on a life of their own and spread far and wide until, hopefully, they encompass all cultures everywhere. What the United Nations did on December 12, 1948, in ratifying the Universal Declaration on Human Rights was to set in motion a tool more important than either paper money or the wheel, one that could lead to the amelioration of suffering and the brotherhood/sisterhood of humanity. Let us now turn to the importance of human rights.

The Significance of Human Rights

In order to counter this tendency to treat "rights" as second-class citizens in our moral repertoire, Joel Feinberg uses a thought experiment in which he asks you to imagine a place, Nowheresville, that is quite nice but lacks rights. Having all the other benefits a good society could offer except this one thing, Feinberg argues, leaves Nowheresville in bad shape, for rights are logically connected with claims. In Nowheresville people cannot make moral claims, and in this way they are deprived of a certain self-respect and dignity. Rights are valid moral claims that give us inherent dignity:

> Having rights, of course makes claiming possible, but it is claiming that gives rights their special moral significance. This feature of rights is connected in a way with the customary rhetoric about what it means to be a human being. Having rights enables us to 'stand up like men,' to look others in the eye, and to feel in some fundamental way the equal of anyone. To think of oneself as the holder of rights is not to be unduly but properly proud, to have that minimal self-respect that is necessary to be worthy of the love and esteem of others. To respect a person then, or to think of him as possessed of human dignity, simply is to think of him as a potential maker of claims.[20]

As such, rights are necessary to an adequate moral theory.

According to the 2000 *United Nations Development Report,* one-fifth of the world, about 1.2 billion people, lives in dire poverty. Half the world lives on less than $1 per day. While 61 percent of Americans, almost 200 million people, are overweight, 170 million people in the third world are seriously underweight. Most of these are children, who, if they fail to receive adequate nourishment, will either die or suffer brain damage.[21] Americans raised more than $1.3 billion for relief of the families of victims of the terrorist attacks on September 11, 2001. Three hundred fifty-three million dollars was raised for the families of the four hundred police officers and firefighters who died trying to save others. The latter comes to $880,000 for each family, families that would have been adequately provided for by city and state pension and insurance plans. Further, the Red Cross decided to provide financial aid (the equivalent of three months' rent) plus money for utilities and groceries, for anyone living in the lower Manhattan area who claimed to have been affected by the destruction of the World Trade Center. It set up card tables in the lobbies of expensive apartment buildings in Tribeca, where wealthy financiers, stock brokers, lawyers, and rock stars live, to offer the residents these financial donations. The higher their income, the larger the financial award; some got as much as $10,000. Meanwhile, three hundred thousand children in other parts of the world die every day of hunger and preventable diseases. Oxfam International is not overwhelmed with financial support for its work.[22]

Article 25(1) of the UN Universal Declaration on Human Rights declares a basic right to adequate food, shelter, and medical care:

> Everyone has the right to a standard of living adequate for the health and well-being of himself and of his family, including food, clothing, housing and medical care and necessary social services, and the right to security in the event of unemployment, sickness, disability, widowhood, old age or other lack of livelihood in circumstances beyond his control.

Hunger and malnutrition are not necessary. The United States alone produces enough food to feed the whole world several times over. There are problems of transporting food to those in need, but a more pressing problem is the loss of food value due to feeding factory-farmed animals. Over 96 percent of the food grown in the United States is fed to animals, mainly in cruel animal factories. The animals, in the form of meat, are eaten by humans, with the resulting loss of about 80 percent of the original food value. For example, we lose about 90 percent of the original food value by eating beef instead of the grains used for feeding cattle. If we became vegetarians, we could feed the world. If we ate the grains fed to factory-farmed animals instead of the animals, we'd preserve enormous amounts of nutrition. The irony of the matter is that Americans are increasingly obese, while people in other parts of the world famish. Basic moral principles upon which the right to an adequate diet is based do not require extreme sacrifice, but they do require that we take reasonable steps to live as good stewards with our resources, doing as much good as possible to mitigate suffering and promote human flourishing. The human rights agenda obligates us "to live simply that others may simply live." As noted above, as a society grows in affluence and education, so do the depth and breadth of its responsibilities to promote human rights, for human rights are simply the realizations of the moral rules. As Jesus said, "To him to whom much has been given, of him will much be required" (Luke 12:48). There are great violations of human rights in the world. People are murdered, die unnecessarily of starvation, are raped and tortured, and even enslaved. Morality requires that we improve these conditions. First of all, each one of us individually has an obligation to do what we can to make sacrifices and donate to international charities; but we also have an obligation to support the building of better institutions that will become the vehicles of human rights.

The point is, the world is shrinking. We are all interconnected, so that economically and socially, we cannot simply do one thing without setting other things in motion. We effect change—for good and bad. Witness this report by Henry Shue on the effects of capitalist strategies on an African community.

A large tract of land in a rural village of an African country has been the property of a peasant family for generations. The family is comparatively well off but not rich. They grow black beans on the land, which is the main source of nourishment and protein in the village. The family employs six workers during the harvest.

One day a man from the capital offers this peasant a contract that not only guarantees him annual payments for a ten-year lease on his land but also guarantees him a salary (regardless of how the crops turned out) to be the foreman for a new kind of production on his land. The new kind of production requires him to grow coffee instead of black beans. Other families accept similar contracts and the production of coffee, to be exported to Europe and the United States, replaces black beans throughout the region.

With the reduction in the supply, the price of black beans skyrockets, so that people cannot afford to buy the nutrient-rich food as they had in the past. When a famine came one season, children and the elderly became weak and many died.[23]

This illustrates how, through no one's direct fault, free-market mechanisms can result in tragedy. The question is, What should be done about it? Should capitalism be restrained? Should the richer countries come to the aid of the poor sub-Saharan region that now finds itself in dire poverty, unable to survive without input from the outside?

As Shue points out, the malnutrition resulting from the choices made in switching from black beans to coffee was not a natural disaster but a social disaster. Specific human decisions, permitted by the presence of specific social institutions and the absence of others in the context of scarcity of land upon which to grow food, resulted in the malnutrition. The Nobel Prize–winning economist Amartya Sen has supported this thesis, arguing that in these sorts of circumstances, changing market conditions have led to mass starvation. Famines are often caused not by a lack of food, but by unfavorable market conditions that cause the poor to be financially unable to procure available food.[24]

Shue puts forth a tripartite set of moral principles to cover such cases of subsistence.

We have:

1. Duties not to eliminate a person's only available means of subsistence—duties to *avoid* depriving.
2. Duties to protect people against deprivation of the only available means of subsistence by other people—duties to *protect* from deprivation.
3. Duties to provide for the subsistence of those unable to provide for their own—duties to *aid* the deprived.

In Shue's account, the state should have had regulations prohibiting such contracts as were entered into by the capitalist and the peasant. But once they have been entered into and disaster strikes, the rest of us are bound by principle 3—a duty to come to the aid of the deprived people of the region and alleviate the malnutrition problem.

Shue doesn't discuss the issue of personal responsibility in such cases, but one might ask whether the peasant and the people of the region aren't responsible for the choices they made in permitting and making contracts to switch crops from black bean to coffee. Let us concede that we have a tripartite duty to try to *avoid*, *protect*, and *aid* in defeating malnutrition in poorer countries. The duty we have is a prima facie duty that can be overridden by other duties, such as a duty to one's own country or more deserving poor people. At some point, the people of the region must take responsibility for their plight, become better educated and live with the consequences of their decisions.

If this is correct, justice, and not merely beneficence, requires that we help the poor who are suffering. Meeting needs, such as in bringing aid to famine victims and people suffering from malnutrition, is not a perfect duty that requires us to aid the people in this region, but an imperfect one. It is an imperfect duty arising from our common humanity. That is, we have a duty arising from benevolence to bring aid to the needy, but because many groups need our aid and we can help only some of them, we may use discretion as to which of the poor are most deserving of our help in the present circumstances.

In a world with surplus wealth and enormous waste, however, it seems cruel and selfish not to ameliorate the staggering suffering brought on by extreme poverty, malnutrition, and disease. Can we go so far as to say that the poor in general have a right to some of our surplus wealth? This leads us to the ideal of cosmopolitanism.

Notes

1. See Johannes Morsink, *The Universal Declaration of Human Rights: Origins, Drafting, and Intent* (Philadelphia: University of Pennsylvania Press, 1999), chap. 1. This is the authoritative work on the development of the Universal Declaration of Human Rights. I am greatly indebted to it. Unfortunately, it has no index.

2. Ibid., introduction.

3. Ibid.

4. The American Anthropological Association position paper 1947, quoted in ibid.

5. For a development of these ideas, see my *Ethics: Discovering Right and Wrong* (Belmont, CA: Wadsworth, 2002).

6. Morsink, *The Universal Declaration of Human Rights*, p. 22.

7. Ibid., pp. 61–65. The amendments were invariably voted down.

8. Maurice Cranston, "Human Rights: Real and Supposed," in *Political Theory and the Rights of Man*, edited by D. D. Raphael (Bloomington: Indiana University Press, 1967); *What Are Human Rights?* (New York: Tapinger, 1973).

9. For a more comprehensive treatment of the nature of a right, see Carl Wellman, *A Theory of Rights: Persons under Laws, Institutions, and Morals* (Totowa, NJ: Rowman and Allanheld, 1985); L. W. Sumner, *The Moral Foundation of Rights* (New York: Oxford University Press, 1987); and James Nickel, *Making Sense of Human Rights: Philosophical Reflections on the Universal Declaration of Human Rights* (Berkeley and Los Angeles: University of California Press, 1987).

10. J. L. Mackie, "Can There Be a Right-Based Moral Theory?" *Midwest Studies in Philosophy* 3 (1978): 355.

11. Michael Rubiner, "Retirement Fever," *New York Times*, February 1996.

12. Jeremy Bloom, "Show Us the Money," *New York Times*, August 1, 2003.

13. See Carl Wellman, *The Proliferation of Rights: Moral Progress or Empty Rhetoric?* (Boulder, CO: Westview, 1999) for a penetrating, balanced discussion of these points. I have been aided by Wellman's work.

14. John Locke, *Second Treatise of Government* (1689), no. 6.

15. Alan Gewirth, *Reason and Morality* (Chicago: University of Chicago Press, 1978); "Epistemology of Human Rights" in *Human Rights*, edited by Ellen Frankel Paul, Jeffrey Paul, and Fred D. Miller Jr. (New York: Blackwell, 1984); and *Human Rights: Essays on Justification and Applications* (Chicago: University of Chicago Press, 1982).

16. Richard Rorty, *Contingency, Irony, and Solidarity* (New York: Cambridge University Press, 1989), p. 63.

17. Jack Donnelly, *Universal Human Rights in Theory and Practice* (Ithaca, NY: Cornell University Press, 1989).

18. John R. Searle, *The Construction of Social Reality* (New York: Free Press, 1995), p. 43. I am indebted to Morton Winston for bringing Searle's theory, as it applies to human rights, to my attention.

19. Ibid., p. 93.

20. Joel Feinberg, "The Nature and Value of Rights," *Journal of Value Inquiry* (1970); reprinted in L. Pojman, ed., *Political Philosophy: Modern and Contemporary Readings* (New York: McGraw-Hill, 2002).

21. *United Nations Development Report* (New York: Oxford University Press, 2000) and World Bank, *World Development Report 2002* (New York: Oxford University Press, 2002).

22. For a good discussion of these discrepancies, see Peter Singer, *One World: The Ethics of Globalization* (New Haven, CT: Yale University Press, 2002), chap. 5. I am indebted to Singer's work for calling my attention to these facts.

23. The illustration is based on Henry Shue, *Basic Rights* (Princeton, NJ: Princeton University Press, 1980), pp. 42f. Shue writes, "The story contains no implication that the man from the capital or the peasant-turned-foreman were malicious or intended to do anything worse than single-mindedly pursue their own respective interests. But the outsider's offer of the contract was another causal factor in producing the maldistribution that would probably persist, barring protective intervention, for at least the decade the contract was to be honored. If the families in the village had rights to subsistence, their rights were being violated. Society, acting presumably by way of the government, ought to protect such families and villages from a severe type of harm that eliminates their ability to feed themselves."

24. Amartya Sen, *Poverty and Famines: An Essay on Entitlement and Deprivation* (New York: Oxford University Press, 1981).

Conclusion

SEPTEMBER 11, 2001, AND subsequent terrorist attacks have changed America and the world. We have been shocked out of our complacency, disabused of our illusion of invulnerability, and forced to face global terrorism. I have argued that the Day of Ignominy may become the Day of Opportunity if we use it to take countermeasures to terrorism and the causes of terrorism and to begin to ameliorate the oppression and injustice in our nation and the world, building a world ruled by international law and peaceful cooperation, and committed to defending universal human rights. I have outlined some short-term and long-term strategies, the most ambitious and controversial of which is a version of institutional cosmopolitanism—world government, which I would base on secular rational morality. World government may also be a fitting response to the growing pressures of globalism. I have also noted, but not developed as fully as I would like, the virtues of nationalism in its ability to develop the opportunities for the close personal relationships and loyalties so vital for personal identity. Some form of nationalism may always be part of the human psyche, though it may be a less all-encompassing variety than what we now experience, a soft nationalism. It will be balanced by a soft form of cosmopolitanism, either informally worked out between nations or by a formal world government that would still encourage and promote individual nation-state autonomy within its domain. One way or another, increased peace and international cooperation will be necessary as we become better-educated people who live in a global village, where actions in Bosnia, South Africa, or the island of Timor affect people in Siberia, Buenos Aires, and Los Angeles. However it happens and whatever the exact result in terms of formal structure or lack thereof, the process should encapsulate Charles Darwin's cosmopolitan vision of an expanding moral circle:

> As man advances in civilization, and small tribes are united into larger communities, the simplest reason would tell each individual that he ought to extend his social instincts and sympathies to all the members of the same nation, though personally unknown to him. This point being once reached, there is only an artificial barrier to prevent his sympathies extending to the men of all nations and races. If, indeed, such men are separated from him by greater differences in appearance or habits, experience unfortunately shows us how long it is, before we look at them as our fellow-creatures. Sympathy beyond the confines of man, that is, humanity to the lower animals, seems to be one of the latest acquisitions. It is apparently unfelt by savages, except towards their pets. How little the old Romans knew of it is shown by their abhorrent gladiatorial exhibitions. The very idea of humanity, as far as I could observe, was new to most of the Gauchos of the Pampas. This virtue, one of the noblest with which man is endowed, seems to arise incidentally from our sympathies becoming more tender and more widely diffused, until they are extended to all sentient beings. As soon as the virtue is honored and practiced by some few men, it spreads through instruction and example to the young, and eventually becomes incorporated in public opinion.[1]

Note

1. Charles Darwin, *The Descent of Man* (1873). Peter Singer, *The Expanding Circle: Ethics and Sociobiology* (Oxford: Oxford University Press, 1983) and Henry Shue, *Basic Rights: Subsistence, Affluence, and U.S. Foreign Policy* (Princeton, NJ: Princeton University Press, 1980) develop this thesis in ways that have influenced my thinking.

About the Author

Louis P. Pojman was Professor of Philosophy Emeritus at the U.S. Military Academy at West Point, New York, and a life member of Clare Hall, Cambridge University. He received his D. Phil. from Oxford University. Dr. Pojman was the author or editor of more than thirty books and one hundred articles in a variety of fields, including philosophy of religion, ethics, epistemology, theories of justice and human nature, and political philosophy, which have been adopted in classrooms across the United States and abroad.

CPSIA information can be obtained at www.ICGtesting.com
Printed in the USA
BVOW02*2352260116

434384BV00007B/78/P